The Thames

FROM THE SOURCE TO THE SEA

Text by Paul Atterbury
Photographs by Anthony Haines

Weidenfeld & Nicolson
London

First published in Great Britain in 1998 by Weidenfeld & Nicolson

Text copyright © Paul Atterbury, 1998
Photographs copyright © Anthony Haines, 1998
The moral right of Paul Atterbury and Anthony Haines to be identified as the authors
of this work has been asserted in accordance with the Copyright, Designs and Patents
Act of 1988
Design and layout and map copyright © Weidenfeld & Nicolson, 1998

A CIP catalogue record for this book is available from the British Library
ISBN 0 297 82414 7

Designed by: Paul Cooper
Map created by: Advanced Illustration
Printed and Bound in: Italy
Set in: Berling Roman

Weidenfeld & Nicolson
The Orion Publishing Group Ltd
Orion House
5 Upper Saint Martin's Lane
London WC2H 9EA

ENDPAPERS: Thames reflections at Henley.

HALF-TITLE PAGE: 'Father Thames' by the Italian sculptor Raphaelle Monti, shown at
the Great Exhibition in 1851, and now on display beside St John's Lock, Lechlade.

FRONTISPIECE: At Cliveden, near Maidenhead, the beech woods sweep down to the
river's edge, delightful scenery accessible only by boat or on foot.

CONTENTS

PHOTOGRAPHER'S NOTES AND ACKNOWLEDGEMENTS

The first time I ever visited the Thames was when I attended the Henley Royal Regatta. Since then I have photographed this area many times, initially concentrating on the mid-section between Windsor and Oxford. My most important influence was the Victorian Henry Taunt, who photographed the Thames in black and white, documenting its many famous landmarks.

The camera I used was a Nikon F3. I used a 50mm lens for the majority of the photographs and occasionally a 135mm or a 28mm lens. A sturdy tripod was required for the night shots where the camera shutter speed could be anything up to fifteen seconds. Very little specialized camera equipment was used. One of the most important aspects of producing these images was the ability to stay in one place for a long period of time waiting for the sun to come out from behind the numerous clouds.

As most of the photographs were taken when walking along the towpath the most important accessories were a good pair of walking shoes, a strong pair of lungs and, in the summer especially, a bottle of water.

I am very grateful to Weidenfeld & Nicolson for giving me the opportunity to travel up and down the Thames, experiencing its many characteristics and meeting the interesting people who live by, work on and visit this historic river. I would also like to thank the following in particular:

The Sports Council, who allowed me to take the photograph of Bisham Abbey (page 69 'owned by English Sports Council, one of the National Sports Centres').

Sheerness Docks whose help was invaluable, and especially Maria Clarke.

Lois Howard for guidance on the best position to take photographs from Winter Hill.

Stephen Oram who allowed me to take the view over Cricklade from the bell-tower in Cricklade church, and the rectors of Abingdon and Lechlade churches for their assistance.

The National Trust for permitting me to take a picture of the Thames from their land.

Jackie Cains for her time and patience in driving me to some of the locations photographed.

ANTHONY HAINES

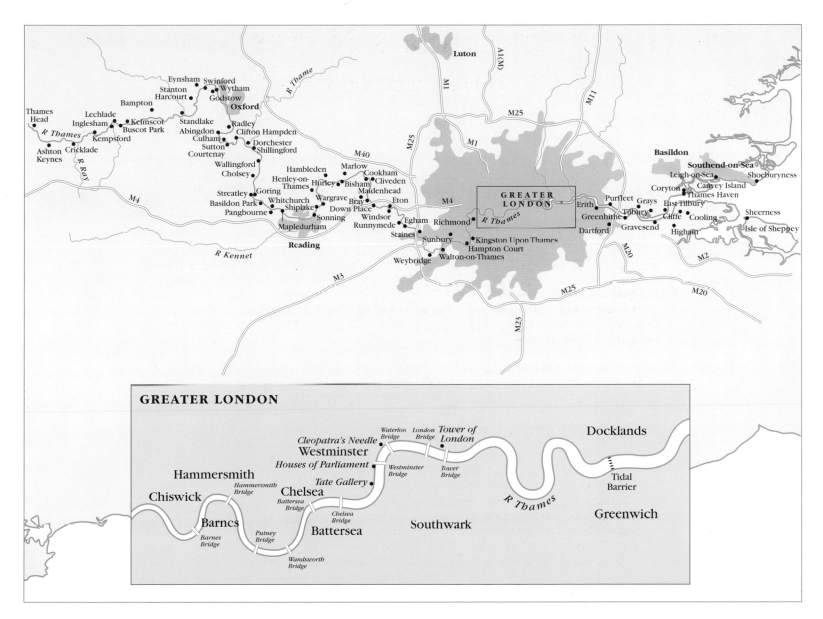

Luton

R Thame

M1

M1(M)

M11

M25

M1

GREATER
LONDON

R Thames

M40

M25

M25

M4

M4

M23

M3

R Kennet

R Ray

R Thames

Eynsham
Swinford
Stanton Wytham
Harcourt Godstow
Bampton   **Oxford**
Thames   Lechlade   Standlake
Head   Inglesham Kelmscot   Radley
Kempsford Buscot Park Abingdon Clifton Hampden
Ashton Cricklade   Culham Dorchester
Keynes   Sutton Shillingford
              Courtenay
            Wallingford   Hambleden   Marlow
            Cholsey   Henley-on-   Cookham
                           Thames Hurley Cliveden
            Streatley Goring   Bisham Maidenhead
            Basildon Park Whitchurch Wargrave Bray
            Pangbourne Shiplake   Down Place Eton
                Mapledurham Sonning Windsor
                              Runnymede Egham Richmond
                Reading   Staines Sunbury
                        Weybridge Walton-on-Thames
                                Kingston Upon Thames
                                Hampton Court

Basildon
            Southend-on-Sea
        Leigh-on-Sea
    Coryton   Canvey Island
Erith Purfleet Thames Haven
      Grays East Tilbury Shoeburyness
Greenhithe Tilbury Cliffe Cooling
  Dartford Gravesend Higham Sheerness
                        Isle of Sheppey

M20

M20

M2

GREATER LONDON

Cleopatra's Needle *Waterloo* *London* Tower of
          Bridge *Bridge* London   **Docklands**
Westminster
Houses of Parliament *Westminster* *Tower*
Hammersmith   *Bridge* *Bridge*
        Tate Gallery
Chiswick *Hammersmith* **Chelsea**   R Thames   **Tidal**
        Bridge *Battersea*   **Barrier**
              Bridge
    Barnes   *Chelsea*   **Southwark**   **Greenwich**
        Putney *Bridge* **Battersea**
    Barnes *Bridge*
    Bridge
          Wandsworth
          Bridge

7

INTRODUCTION

Colourful boats for hire at Henley.

The Thames is England's greatest river. It flows for over two hundred miles across the heart of the country, from the Jurassic limestone of the Cotswolds to the clays of the London basin and the estuary in a broad valley formed over millions of years and completed by the last phase of the Ice Age. Populated since the Stone Age, the Thames valley has also been at the heart of English history. The Romans were probably the first to recognize the river's strategic and cultural importance and several of their major roads, Watling Street, the Fosse Way, Ermine Street and the Icknield Way, were associated with it. Roman fortifications, settlements and villas were scattered along the valley from Cirencester to the estuary, and it was the Romans who gave the river its name, Tamesis, a combination of Isis, the old name for the river from its source to Dorchester, and Thame, the tributary it meets near Dorchester. The Romans were also the first to develop the Thames as a major trade route, laying down in London the foundations of what was to become the largest port in the world, and establishing the river's economic importance.

The Saxons invaded England along the Thames, the Normans built major fortresses along its banks and in subsequent centuries the defence of the Thames against European invasion was always a priority. The Tudors and the Stuarts greatly expanded the defences, building new forts and dockyards, but the Dutch still managed to sail up the Thames and the Medway in 1667. More fortifications were built in the nineteenth century and as late as 1940 the Thames was turned into a fortified line of defence by the building of a chain of pillboxes and strong points. The German invasion never took place but German bombers flew along the Thames on their way to attack London.

The geographic importance of the Thames also inspired the Christian church, and from the tenth century abbeys, monasteries, convents and other religious institutions grew up along the valley and, until the dissolution of the monasteries under Henry VIII, played a major role in its economic development. The secular world then took over, with royal palaces and great houses being built by the river's banks. The commercial exploitation of the river had been started by the Romans, but it was in the Middle Ages that fishing and milling became major industries. The Thames always held an abundance of fish. Trout, salmon, eels and, nearer the estuary, shrimps, cockles and even lobsters were so plentiful that they formed the staple diet for everyone living by the river. By the eighteenth century the variety and quantity of fish had been greatly diminished by pollution, but as late as 1784 a 30lb salmon was caught by London Bridge, and eels were still being taken by the bucketful. Fishermen and millers were always in dispute about their conflicting water needs and from the Middle Ages weirs and other methods of controlling the water were being built. These in turn outraged the bargemen, whose trade was dependent upon a good and regular flow of water. Boats were hauled upstream by teams of men and horses, often struggling through the shallows caused by weirs and mill streams, and even the downstream passage with the river's flow was hazardous and unpredictable.

However, the importance of river transport was such that improvements were gradually made to it and by the seventeenth century, when the first locks were built, the Thames had become a major navigation route. In the late eighteenth century canals were built to join the Thames, linking London by water to the Midlands, to Bristol and the Severn and to the south coast, and turning the river into a major artery and the centre of a radiating network of navigable waterways. At the same time, London's docks were developed. Transport on the river remained important through the nineteenth century but it was steadily undermined by the railways. The rapid growth of road transport after the First World War really brought to an end river transport in commercial terms and the subsequent decline of the docks was hastened by an increase in the size of ships and radical changes in methods of cargo handling. The coming of the container brought an end to inland ports, but the Thames kept its hold on international maritime trade through the new docks at Tilbury and Sheerness.

The Thames is many things: a country stream, a rural river in a delightful landscape, a powerful waterway winding its way through history, a grand and majestic tideway, and each has its particular quality and appeal. The Thames is a royal river, inseparable from centuries of the monarchy, and at the same time it is inextricably interwoven with the complex strands of church and state that form the history of England. London is the Thames, and yet the river has many other lives that have nothing to do with the capital city. It is a line through the heart of England, an exploration of the rich diversity of the English landscape and the wealth of English architecture from the Normans to Post-Modernism.

The appeal of the Thames is universal, notably to artists and writers. In the seventeenth century the great etcher Hollar was the first to depict in detail London's river and its architecture in his broad panoramas and vistas. Eighty years later Canaletto brought the river to life and at the same time Hogarth, Thornhill and the marine painter Scott painted aspects of it. In 1732, the three of them travelled from Billingsgate to Greenwich and back, exploring the river as a source of inspiration. Later, it was the turn of the watercolourists, Girtin, De Wint and above all else Turner, who is reported to have said of the Thames: 'There is finer scenery on its banks than any river in Italy.' In the nineteenth century Stansfield, Roberts and particularly Whistler captured the atmosphere of London's river, while at the end of that century the main contribution was made by French artists, Tissot, Monet and Derain. The Thames flows equally through literature, from Chaucer, Shakespeare, Ben Jonson and Spenser to Pope, Hood, Thompson, Gray, Wordsworth and Dickens.

Today, the Thames is most familiar as a source of leisure and entertainment. Nearly all the traffic on the river is a reflection of this; from the punts, canoes and skiffs of the upper reaches, to the motor boats and cabin cruisers that fill the locks and the most popular stretches, the pleasure and trip boats that ply up and

The *Queen Mary*, a former Glasgow passenger vessel now moored by Waterloo Bridge as a floating restaurant and bar, brings life to London's river.

down London's river, and the dinghies and sailing boats of the estuary. On a summer weekend in any popular stretch boats fill the water, fishermen line the banks and walkers and strollers take up the towpath – the three activities existing in an uneasy harmony. At the same time, any riverside pub will be bursting, even though they no longer offer the eleven-course fish dinners that Dickens so enjoyed. Somehow, the river absorbs it all, and still offers relaxation to all who seek it. It was the Victorians who started all this, and the Edwardians who developed it into a fine art.

The Thames was at the heart of England's new-found enthusiasm for holidays and relaxation, thanks in part to its proximity to London. Outings on the river by day, or leisurely weekends in the expanding network of smart riverside hotels, became increasingly fashionable. Goring, Pangbourne, Hurley and Maidenhead were towns and villages that hitherto had seen few visitors, but quickly grew into well-known resorts. Contemporary guides are full of advertisements describing ideal holiday centres, cruises on the glorious Thames and hotels in unrivalled positions. They even claimed resort status for unexpected places like Reading.

Charles Dickens referred, in the 1880s, to the new fashion for camping by the river, one that he found rather hard to understand. However, the great enthusiasm for this was underlined by the success of books like *Three Men in a Boat* and *The Wind in the Willows*. The enormous growth of Thames-based leisure activities in late Victorian England was also due to those railway companies whose routes served the river. The Great Western, for example, offered excursions, anglers' tickets, cheap tickets for picnic and pleasure parties and facilities for the transport, on passenger trains, of horses and carriages, bicycles, and even boats and canoes.

The pursuit of leisure dominates the Thames today, but this is just another phase in the centuries of history carried easily by the sinuous curves and sweeping bends of England's most glorious river.

THAMES HEAD TO OXFORD

The upper reaches of the Thames are secret and delightful, and their exploration, now made easy by the Thames Path, offers an unusual introduction to the landscape and architecture of Gloucestershire and the Cotswolds. In some ways these are familiar, but their particular blend of gentle wooded hills and golden stone buildings is made more enjoyable by the intimate and domestic nature of the course of the river. Rising to the south-west of Cirencester, in an area settled both in prehistory and by the Romans, the Thames, at first often invisible for some distance, then follows a private, wandering route through quiet farmland. It passes near to, but manages to avoid, all villages until Ashton Keynes, by which time it has become a well-defined stream.

The first significant place is Cricklade, an old-fashioned market town that the river almost misses, and then, as the broad valley takes shape between the distant lines of hills, the Thames, by now a little river, pursues a remote and winding route towards Inglesham and Lechlade. Here navigation begins and the river comes of age, with pleasure cruisers working through the locks that were originally built to make it part of the commercial waterway network that served England's industry and agriculture at the end of the eighteenth century.

Old bridges, remote locks and pretty stone villages with riverside inns, handsome churches and old manors of the kind loved by William Morris maintain the river's traditional atmosphere all the way to Oxford. Many hidden features of the upper Thames are made accessible through leisurely explorations by boat, on foot or by bicycle, for example the abbeys, monasteries and convents that were associated with the river, the early mills, flash locks and ferries, the abandoned canals and railways and the impact of the river upon artists and writers.

Near Thames Head

A degree of uncertainty has always surrounded the exact source of the Thames. Traditionally, there have been two main claimants: Seven Springs, north of Cirencester, now generally accepted as the source of the Churn, a rival that joins the Thames near Cricklade; and Thames Head, adjacent to Trewsbury Camp, an Iron Age hillfort north of Kemble and near the Roman Fosse Way. Thames Head is a quiet and secret place, with the source, which is dry for much of the year, marked by a simple monument and a small stone circle, said to be a Roman well. The best way to trace the first meanderings of the infant river, which is often dry and thus virtually invisible above the little village of Ewen, is to follow the Thames Path, which starts its 178 mile route to Woolwich at Thames Head. Far more apparent is the long abandoned Thames & Severn Canal, whose grassy bed crosses the fields near Thames Head.

Cricklade from the Church Tower

Cricklade is a small market town dominated by the richly decorated and pinnacled tower of St Sampson's, a great Cotswold wool church built from the same stone as Gloucester cathedral. This view from the tower looks out across the churchyard and the typical sixteenth- and seventeenth-century stone houses, with their gables and mullioned windows, towards the Thames which flows through the trees beyond the houses. Perhaps established by King Alfred the Great as a fortified strongpoint during his battles with the Danes, Cricklade is a quiet and pleasant town with a rich history. At the time of King Ethelred there was a mint here, and some of the silver pennies it produced are in the local museum. A Norman church, a medieval priory, a seventeenth-century school and plenty of typical Cotswold stone buildings add to the town's traditional atmosphere.

The Rural Thames near Cricklade

From its source, the Thames follows a quiet and undramatic route across the low-lying landscape of fields broken by hedges and woodland. It wanders around several small villages, growing gradually from a stream into a little river, big enough in centuries past to feed several mills around the village of Somerford Keynes, whose church has a Saxon doorway and unusual eleventh-century carvings. Next is Ashton Keynes, the first village actually on the river, and now surrounded by the 12,000 acres of wetlands and flooded gravel pits that make up the Cotswold Water Park.

For its first few miles the Thames is a delightfully rural river, whose shallow waters add interest to a quintessentially English landscape, seen here at its best in the long shadows of a summer evening, between Cricklade and Castle Eaton.

Distant View of Inglesham Church

The Thames winds past Castle Eaton and Kempsford, villages blessed with interesting churches. St Mary's at Castle Eaton is crowned with a little bellcote, set up during the restoration work carried out by William Butterfield, the great Victorian Gothic revivalist architect. Kempsford, formerly the home of the Plantagenets, has a magnificent church tower apparently built for John of Gaunt in 1390. This is the only English church with an Irish peer buried beneath the organ. From Kempsford a minor road crosses the river to lead southwards to seventeenth-century Hannington Hall. From here, the river forms the boundary between Gloucestershire and Wiltshire, exploring a remote landscape of scattered farms on its way to Inglesham. Seen across the water meadows, this once great wool village is now just a church and a few cottages.

Inglesham Church

One of the great treasures of the Thames valley is the little eleventh-century church of St John the Baptist at Inglesham. Described as 'a stony, lichen-crusted country church among the whispering grasses' and formerly associated with a priory, it now stands in delightful isolation beside the river. Inside the church box pews, an Anglo-Saxon sculpture of the Virgin Mary, fragments of medieval wall paintings and a sense of quiet decay generate a remarkably peaceful atmosphere. The church's original condition is due largely to the efforts of William Morris, who loved it and fought to save it from the elaborate restoration schemes so beloved by Victorian architects. His determination to protect England's architectural heritage led him to found the Society for the Protection of Ancient Buildings, and the saving of Inglesham in 1888 was one of the Society's first triumphs.

The Thames & Severn Canal

Across the river from Inglesham, overgrown and half-hidden by trees, there is a round tower. This is one of the characteristic lock-keeper's houses of the old Thames & Severn Canal, a waterway completed in 1789 as part of an ambitious inland navigation link between London and Gloucester and Bristol via the river Severn. Never a great commercial success, the Thames & Severn Canal struggled on until the early years of this century. Abandoned from the 1930s, the ruined canal has long remained a romantic monument to eighteenth-century canal mania. Now the subject of a long term restoration project, the canal's route makes an excellent walk along the Golden Valley to Stroud, and beyond. The round house at Inglesham marks the site of the canal's first lock, and its junction with the Thames. From here its route runs parallel to the river for some miles before swinging north towards Cirencester and the great Sapperton tunnel, which at 3,817 yards is one of the longest in Britain.

Oxbow Bends near Lechlade

With the opening of the Thames & Severn Canal the Thames became navigable as far as Inglesham, and small craft today can still reach the site of the former junction. However, Lechlade's handsome Halfpenny Bridge of 1792 is effectively the start of the navigable Thames, and it was by this bridge that the canal company had its wharves and warehouses. Lechlade is a generous town of golden grey stone, spreading northwards from the river, and a pleasant base for visits to the upper Thames and its attractions, such as nearby Buscot Park, now owned by the National Trust. Between the town and the first lock, St John's, the Thames, now a river of some substance, winds through its water meadows in a series of gentle oxbow bends, dwarfed by the wide expanse of its valley.

Lechlade's Monuments

The broad valley of the Thames
is dominated for miles around by
the elegant spire of St Lawrence's
church. Carried on a typical
battlemented tower, it was
described by Shelley as an 'aerial
pile' whose pinnacles were 'like
pyramids of fire'. Impressive from
all directions, the sixteenth-
century church is best seen from
the river, a natural landmark for
those entering Lechlade from the
south. Equally hard to miss for
those on boats or walking the
towpath is the concrete pillbox,
one of a series built in 1940 along
the route of the Thames to turn
the river into a fortified line of
defence against the projected
German invasion. Still
indestructible, but softened by
time, this is now quite rightly
taking its place in the broad
canvas of more recent history.

St John's Lock, Lechlade

Although used as a navigation
route at least since Roman times,
boats on the Thames had until
the eighteenth century a difficult
passage because of the many
private weirs and barriers and the
water shortages caused by
extraction by mill owners. The
first modern lock was built in
1630, at Swift Ditch near
Abingdon, and from that date
onwards navigation was steadily
improved. By the end of the
eighteenth century the river's
route was properly controlled by
locks and, with its various canal
connections, the Thames became
the backbone of an extensive
waterway network, much of
which still survives today.
St John's is the first lock on the
Thames, and its small
dimensions, characteristic of all
those north of Oxford, can
clearly be seen, along with the
recumbent stone statue of Father
Thames, carved for the Great
Exhibition of 1851, and installed
beside the lock in 1974 following
a period of duty marking the
source at Thames Head.

Kelmscot Manor

In 1871 William Morris and his wife Jane, accompanied by their artist friend Dante Gabriel Rossetti, abandoned London and moved to Kelmscot Manor beside the Thames. A typical sixteenth-century Cotswold asymmetrical house in golden stone and marked by a profusion of gables and steep stone roofs, it became the prototype for a whole generation of English country houses built in the vernacular traditions so enjoyed by Arts and Crafts architects and designers. Morris lived at Kelmscot until his death in 1896 and the house became his 'Earthly Paradise', his Utopia in his *News from Nowhere*. He loved his Thames-side house:

Kelmscot Manor has come to me to be the type of the pleasant places of the earth, and of the homes of harmless people not overburdened with the intricacies of life; and as others love the race of man through their lovers or their children, so I love the earth through that small space of it.

William Morris' Tomb, Kelmscot

After Morris' death in 1896, his body was carried on a simple, flower-decorated farmcart to Kelmscot church and buried in the graveyard near his manor, beneath a tomb designed by his great friend, Philip Webb. Strikingly simple, and echoing in its style both the powerful forms and geometry of Webb's architecture and furniture, and the roof shapes of vernacular buildings, the tomb is now a gentle, lichen-covered monument to a great Victorian. Morris lies with his wife Jane beside the river he knew so well, and loved so deeply:

*See, we have left our hopes and
    fears behind
To give our very hearts up unto
    thee;
What better place than this then
    could we find
By this sweet stream that knows
    not of the sea,
That guesses not the city's misery,
This little stream whose hamlets
    scarce have names,
This far-off, lonely mother of the
    Thames.*

From Swinford Bridge

Beyond Kelmscot the Thames wanders through a broad valley broken by clumps, trees and remote villages and brought to life by the fluctuating population of pleasure boaters. Some of the river's oldest bridges are best seen from a boat, notably the three arches at Radcot, two of which date from 1280 while the central one is younger, having been rebuilt in 1387 following a battle between Henry Bolinbroke and the Earl of Oxford. Nearly as old are the six arches of Newbridge, spanning the river since the thirteenth century and separating the two famous inns, the Maybush and the Rose Revived. This bridge was also the site of a battle, a Civil War skirmish in 1644, one of several in the area as the rival armies fought for the control of Oxford. Even less tangible today is a site near Shifford where Alfred the Great is reputed to have held one of the first English parliaments.

Swinford Bridge

The Thames was extensively redeveloped during the eighteenth century, by the building of locks, and by the cutting of new navigation channels to bypass some of the shallows, and the twists and turns of its natural course. At the same time, the local road network was improved, prompting the building of new bridges across the river. Typical is Tadpole Bridge, with its elegant single arch, but far grander is Swinford Bridge, whose classical arches cut from a lovely but rather soft stone – now battered by time and badly driven boats – were completed in 1777 as part of a new turnpike road. Crowned by a fine balustraded parapet, this is still a toll bridge, one of only two left on the river, and a rare link with the way such structures were financed in the eighteenth century.

Stanton Harcourt

Sandwiched between the Thames
and its famous tributary, the
Windrush, Stanton Harcourt is a
remarkable village, built on a site
whose early history is marked by
two standing stones. From the
time of Henry I until the early
eighteenth century, when they
moved to Nuneham Courtenay,
it was the seat of the Harcourt
family, and it is their story that
the village still reflects. The great
manor they built has largely
disappeared, but their legacy is
the extraordinary medieval
kitchen, visible on the left a huge
structure unlike any other of its
period, and eccentric in its lack of
any obvious chimney. Another
Harcourt legacy is the great
tower, in the centre behind the
tree. Here Alexander Pope
completed his translation of the
fifth book of the *Iliad*, and wrote
epitaphs for local lovers. The
third tower, square and bold,
belongs to the cruciform church,
a handsome building that
contains exciting Harcourt tombs.

Evening View near Swinford

Between Lechlade and Oxford
the Thames is rich in literary and
historical associations. Apart from
William Morris, there were other
nineteenth-century writers who
were inspired by the river and its
history. Sir Walter Scott drew
Cumnor and the tragedy of Amy
Robsart into his novel,
Kenilworth, while Matthew
Arnold featured the famous ferry
at Bablock Hythe in his poem,
The Scholar Gypsy. This ferry
has existed since Roman times,
and until the Second World War
it carried vehicles. Now, after
several periods of closure, a
passenger ferry is operating
again, in association with the
adjacent pub.
Out of season, when the boats
and caravans have gone, and the
walkers and the motorists have
left the river banks and the pubs,
and when the river returns to a
state of almost primeval isolation,
its appeal to generations of
writers is easily understood.

The Trout Inn, Godstow

The Thames is famous for its pubs, a number of which are called The Trout. Best known of all, and familiar to generations of Oxford students and, more recently, to families enjoying boating holidays on the river, is The Trout Inn at Godstow. Tucked in beside Godstow Bridge and overlooking the lock, the stone-roofed building was originally part of the nunnery that stood across the river. The elevated route of the Oxford ring road has rather changed the scene since those days but the setting still enjoys a picturesque popularity, thanks in part to its proximity to the city. The distant views over the river are framed by the hills and woods of Wytham, while nearer at hand are the buildings of the university farm, in a distinctive English vernacular style.

Godstow Nunnery

Crumbling walls and battered ruins are all that remain of the famous 'house of Nunnes beside Oxford'. Beautifully sited beside the river, between the abbeys at Eynsham and Osney, the nunnery was built in the twelfth century and finally destroyed in the seventeenth. Godstow is inextricably linked with the story of Rosamund Clifford, the Fair Rosamund of legend and romance. She was educated in the nunnery and there met Henry II, who fell utterly in love with her. He installed her in a mysterious bower by his great palace at Woodstock, protected by an impenetrable maze, and there he visited her in secret. She died soon after and, according to legend, Queen Eleanor may have had a part in her death. Buried at Godstow before the high altar, her tomb became an object of veneration. Later, at the orders of Bishop Hugh, she was reburied elsewhere, in order that 'other women, warned by her example, may refrain from unlawful love'.

OXFORD TO HENLEY

The Thames breaks into a number of streams and waterways as it reaches Oxford but soon after leaving the city it reforms itself into one river, swelled additionally by the waters of the Cherwell, one of the major tributaries. Flanked by distant hills, the river takes a rather indecisive route along the wide valley, swinging in great loops past the woods of Nuneham Park, round Abingdon and Sutton Courtenay, to the south of Dorchester where in the shadow of the Sinodun Hills it meets the Thame, and round Wallingford.

As the valley begins to narrow, a series of smaller meanders then take it past Goring and Pangbourne and into Reading. The narrowing valley creates a more dramatic landscape, with large tracts of woodland on the hillsides breaking up the open fields. Most towns and villages are set back from the river but in one way or another they owe their existence to it, having grown up around a bridge or crossing point, or a major religious institution. A number of grand country houses sit near the river, drawn to it progressively from the seventeenth century by the scenic qualities of the landscape and by the increasing wealth engendered by the Thames, its towns and its associated farmlands.

Since the nineteenth century tourism has also played a role, helped by the spreading network of railways that linked most parts of the river, improved roads, regular steamer services and the proliferation of boatyards and hotels. The Kennet, with its canalized link to Bristol, joins the Thames at Reading, where industrial growth adds another element to the changes that affected the Thames valley in the Victorian period. The river's route from Reading to Henley, past Sonning, Shiplake and Wargrave, is particularly attractive.

Punts and Skiffs at Magdalen Bridge

The Thames separates itself into a number of rivers and streams for its passage through Oxford, with the main channel passing well to the west of the city centre. Oxford's waterways do not, therefore, offer quite the same architectural delights as the famous Cambridge Backs. Despite this, pleasure boating has probably been a popular activity in the city since the founding of the university in the thirteenth century. Skiffs and punts abound, although their centre of activity is actually on the river Cherwell from Magdalen Bridge to its junction with the Thames by Christ Church Meadow. Punting is a traditional Oxford pastime, perennially popular with both students and tourists who struggle to master the difficult technique of propelling, and controlling, the punt using the long pole.

Tom Quad, Christ Church

Most of Oxford's colleges are well away from the river, and it is really only Christ Church that can be fully seen from the water. Founded by Cardinal Wolsey in 1525, the college's splendid stone buildings are ranged round Tom Quad, the great quadrangle that takes its name from the bell known as Great Tom that hangs in the tower above the main entrance, shown here. Coming originally from Osney Abbey, this is one of the largest bells in England. The quadrangle was to have had a cloister built from the flat arches that surround it, but this was never constructed. Across Tom Quad is the tower and spire of Christ Church cathedral, built on the remains of the old convent church of St Frideswide, Oxford's patron saint and a somewhat mythical eighth-century heroine. Mostly twelfth-century, the cathedral also has a remarkable fan-vaulted roof over the choir, one of the great glories of sixteenth-century English Gothic architecture.

Christ Church Meadow

Boating in Oxford has an idyllic quality during the long summer months, much enjoyed by students once the exams are finished. Christ Church Meadow is flanked by two rivers, the Cherwell and the Thames, and a leisurely trip from Magdalen Bridge on the Cherwell to Folly Bridge on the Thames offers enticing views of major Oxford landmarks. Adjacent to Magdalen Bridge is fifteenth-century Magdalen College with its graceful tower, the setting for the singing of the May morning hymn, and nearby are the Botanic Gardens. From here, the Cherwell winds through the trees to its two junctions with the Thames, one its natural course and the other a man-made cut. Typical of the city views from the river, this shows Christ Church College, the spire of the cathedral and, in the background, the distinctive dome of Sir Christoper Wren's Sheldonian Theatre. Its building was inspired by Gilbert Sheldon, Archbishop of Canterbury, who disapproved of plays being performed in St Mary's church.

Oxford's Architecture

Oxford today is a modern, cosmopolitan city with a more interesting blend of 'town and gown' than can be found in Cambridge. However, the traditions and history of the university are so strong and so well established, that inevitably they have always formed the city's core. Oxford is, in architectural terms, a rich city, and most of that architecture has been created by the university. The colleges represent every architectural style used in Britain, from the medieval Gothic of Merton to the modernism of St Catherine's, and in between Tudor and Jacobean, the baroque of Wren, the classicism of the eighteenth century and the Victorian Gothic revival. Over the centuries many types of building material have been used, including stone from local Oxfordshire, Cotswold and Northamptonshire quarries, but most characteristic is the glowing honey-coloured stone shown here, in grand classical formality, at Christ Church.

Oxford Boating

A traditional launch winds its way carefully among the punts on the Cherwell near Magdalen Bridge in a typical Oxford boating scene. Despite strict speed limits, many launches and motor boats are not driven with enough care and consideration, a problem that has afflicted the Thames since the Victorian period. Writing in 1888, Charles Dickens expressed strong, but still relevant views on the subject:

Steam launches are too often the curse of the river. Driving along at an excessive rate of speed, with an utter disregard to the comfort or necessities of anglers, oarsmen and boating parties, the average steam launch engineer is an unmitigated nuisance ... the launches are navigated with a recklessness which is simply shameful. Perhaps the worst offenders are the people who pay their £5 a day for their hire of a launch, and whose idea of a holiday is the truly British notion of getting over as much ground as possible ... especially after the copious lunch which is one of the features of the day's outing.

University Boat Clubs

Competitive rowing has long been a part of university life in Oxford, with Eights Week, the college boat races, taking part at the end of May. This traditional festival is accompanied by the famous college commemoration balls. The racing takes place on the river by Christ Church Meadow, where the river bank is the long-established setting for the university boat clubs. Originally, each college had an ornately decorated barge moored on the river, but these have gradually disappeared, closing the door on a particularly colourful aspect of college life. The boat clubs that now line the bank are far more serious institutions, reflecting the all-year-round nature of modern competitive rowing. From these clubs are drawn the squads for the well-known university boat race between Oxford and Cambridge, held in London each April over a strenuous Thames tideway course between Putney and Mortlake.

Oxford Allotments

The Thames in Oxford is a river of contrasts. Grand buildings of all periods line its banks, bringing to life centuries of history, tradition and great sporting occasions. There are also visible legacies of a much more commercial nature, echoes of a time when the Thames was the backbone of a national waterway artery, thanks to its links to the industrial Midlands via the Oxford Canal. Today this canal, which still creeps into the heart of Oxford, is one of the best-loved leisure waterways in England. At the same time, the Thames is an enjoyably domestic river, winding its way through the Victorian terraces of Osney and other, later housing developments. Even that great British institution, the allotment, now sadly seriously under threat from changing lifestyles and commercial pressures, is an important feature of Thames-side life in Oxford.

Old Bridge by Iffley Lock

South of Oxford, the Thames quickly becomes a rural river once again. Iffley Lock, one of the oldest on the river, is the first outside the city, and its setting is attractive, despite the destruction by fire many years ago of the picturesque mill that used to feature in so many paintings of the area. Iffley is a very old village whose name, according to Charles Dickens, has been spelt over eighty different ways in the last 1,000 years. The best feature of the village is the famous Norman church, grand and substantial with a massive tower, and with a doorway richly decorated with chevron and beakhead patterns and typically Romanesque stylized animals and birds. The great black font is also worth a look, along with the ancient yew in the churchyard. The next lock is Sandford. Another famous mill, of thirteenth-century origins, was situated here and still at work making paper in the 1980s, but has now been replaced by a housing complex with vaguely mill-like detailing.

Bank Clearing near Radley

Although the Thames has a well-established towpath from Lechlade to London, much of which is now the route of the Thames Path, the river's banks are still largely riparian, with their management in the hands of various private owners. Natural growth on the banks is often cleared for a number of reasons, including land management and maintenance for agriculture and bank protection. Water courses around locks need also to be kept clear. However, the most popular reason for the type of bank clearance shown here is to make the river more accessible to the thousands of anglers that regularly line its banks. Throughout much of the length of the non-tidal Thames fishing rights are held by clubs, who look after the stretches in their care for their members. Clearing operations of the kind shown here are often carried out before fishing competitions.

Nuneham Courtney

Early in the eighteenth century the Harcourt family moved from their old manor at Stanton Harcourt to Nuneham Courtney, to build a new house on a magnificent site overlooking a great sweeping bend of the river. There are many fine houses by the Thames, but this is one of the most dramatic. The grandly formal building dates from 1756, with later additions. It is now owned by the university, and the extraordinary collections amassed by the Harcourts have long been removed. However, there is still a landscaped park laid out by Capability Brown complete with grottoes and other curiosities, including the Carfax Conduit. This was erected in Oxford in 1590, removed in 1787 when the High Street was widened, and given a new home at Nuneham. Also removed in the late eighteenth century was the original village of Nuneham Courtney, as Lord Harcourt felt that it spoilt his view. Instead, he constructed a new estate village away to the east, flanking the main Dorchester road, now the A423.

Abingdon

Always an important Thames town because of its bridge, Abingdon became one of the major monastic centres on the river through its great abbey, founded in the seventh century. The abbey disappeared long ago, apart from its gatehouse, following its abolition in 1538, but by that time Abingdon had become a wealthy wool town. By the seventeenth century it was a thriving market town, its standing reflected by the grand and monumental town hall with its open ground floor, designed by one of Wren's city masons. Rather quieter today, Abingdon is still an attractive riverside town. Elegant eighteenth-century houses flank the street that leads from the town hall towards the river and St Helen's church, whose buttressed spire commands the Thames' winding course. This view, from the tower of St Helen's, shows Abingdon's famous medieval bridge and the typical Thames landscape of a lazy river drifting gently through meadows and woodland.

Clifton Hampden Bridge

South of Abingdon, artificial cuts
have straightened the Thames,
putting the villages of Sutton
Courtenay and Long Wittenham
on to quiet backwaters. Both are
traditionally attractive, with fine
churches and other buildings of
interest, notably the twelfth-
century Norman Hall in Sutton
Courtenay. Eric Blair, better
known as George Orwell, is
buried in the churchyard at
Sutton Courtenay.
Clifton Lock ends the second
artificial cut, and not far away are
the six red brick arches of Clifton
Hampden Bridge, a Victorian
Gothic revival structure probably
taking its style from the nearby
church. The church perches on
an unexpected outcrop of rock, a
bold bluff rising from the flat
landscape and sheltering the little
village, with its famous pub The
Barley Mow.

Day's Lock, from the Sinodun Hills

Some of the Thames' locks are
set in delightful spots, quite
isolated from towns and villages.
Typical is Day's, its name a
reminder of those distant times
when locks on the river were
privately built and operated, with
their owners collecting the tolls.
This view down on to the lock
and its weir, set among the
woods, shows well the Thames'
meandering curves through the
soft and domestic landscape of its
valley. Not far from Day's Lock is
Dorchester, another little town
with a great history. In the tenth
century this was the centre of a
huge diocese that included
Worcester, Bath, Lichfield,
Salisbury and Winchester.
Decline was steady from that
date, but a legacy of earlier
importance is the great abbey,
one of the glories of the river,
and the only one of the
numerous major monastic
buildings of the Thames valley to
have survived the Dissolution.

Wallingford Bridge

A town of Roman origins, thanks to the ford that used to cross the river here, Wallingford has enjoyed a colourful history. A castle built by the Normans turned the town into an important stronghold in the medieval period, when it apparently boasted fourteen churches. Three of these survive, notably St Peter's with its curious pierced spire designed by Sir William Blackstone, an eighteenth-century judge buried in the church, who did much to encourage the building of turnpike roads. Many kings and queens stayed in the castle, and it was here in 1153 that Queen Matilda signed the treaty that surrendered her claims to the throne in favour of her heir, the future Henry II. The castle's last moment of glory was during the Civil War, when it was the final stronghold in Oxfordshire to hold out against Cromwell. Finally captured in 1646, it was demolished soon after. Also largely medieval is the stone bridge, whose seventeen arches stride across the water meadows.

Sinodun Hills

Two large, smoothly rounded hills, each surprisingly regular and each crowned by a clump of trees, rise from the low-lying landscape of the Thames valley. The strangely uniform shape is apparent in this view, from Day's Lock. Visible for miles in every direction, the hills have a certain mystical quality, particularly at those times of year when the low sun throws them into sharp relief. It is no surprise to find the remains of an Iron Age hillfort on the top. The Sinodun Hills, or the Wittenham Clumps, as they are known, are a powerful and primitive element in an otherwise domestic and agricultural landscape. A path leads to the top from which there are magnificent views westwards towards the Vale of the White Horse, down across Dorchester and the River Thame, and eastwards along the Thames valley towards the Chilterns.

Near Moulsford

After Dorchester and its junction with the Thame the Thames changes. It becomes a grander river, wide and majestic in a landscape that is also changing. The twists and turns through low-lying meadows in a wide valley bounded by distant hills are replaced by generous sweeping curves into an ever narrowing valley with steep tree-lined sides. It is a more dramatic setting, befitting a major waterway that has now grown to fill its valley. Despite the changes in scale, the river is still remote, with a few small villages and farms set back from the banks. One of these, Moulsford, boasts a little church restored by Gilbert Scott in 1847, the famous pub, the Beetle and Wedge where H. G. Wells wrote *The History of Mr Polly*, and a fine railway bridge by Brunel, its four beautifully proportioned brick arches crossing the river at an angle. The railway from London to Oxford crosses the Thames no less than seven times.

Goring Lock

This busy summer scene illustrates the popularity of Thames cruising, and the variety of craft that use the river for pleasure. Most common are the white fibreglass cabin cruisers, often lavishly equipped for comfortable holidays, direct descendants of the motor cruisers of the 1930s. Generally timber built, and with a natural elegance that modern boat designers seem unable to recapture, these pioneering craft could be hired in the late 1930s for between £7 and £14 per week. The more colourful boat is a modern steel canal cruiser, built along traditional lines and a common visitor to the river from the canal network. The locks on the Thames are manned, and the lock keeper stands outside his cottage, keeping an eye on things. His flowery garden is typical, reflecting the competitive spirit shown towards gardening and lock decoration by the keepers.

Pelmans Old Time Golden Gallopers at Goring Regatta

In an exciting setting in which gently rising hills, broken only by woodland, roll back from the river, the twin villages of Goring and Streatley face each other across the Thames. Formerly picturesque but now rather commuter-bound, they are linked by a road bridge that also marks the crossing point of Icknield Way, the famous prehistoric trackway. A path from here also leads up to the Ridgeway, the greatest trackway in southern England. Right by the river is Goring's church, possibly linked to a former nunnery in the village of which practically nothing remains.

Many regattas are held along the banks of the Thames but, living as they do in the shadow of Henley, most are local affairs supported by entertainments and activities not directly connected with boating.

The Goring Gap

South of Goring the hills close in, forcing the river into a dramatic tree-lined valley that carries it through the Chilterns. With little or no road access the valley can really only be enjoyed by boat or on foot from the Thames Path. The train also offers quite a good view for its route is close to the valley. Basildon bridge at Gatehampton, seen here, carries the line across the mouth of the Gap. This is another design by Brunel, in a more robust and conventional style.

This is an area rich in fine houses. The best is Basildon Park, designed by John Carr of York and built in 1767 for Sir Francis Sykes, for whom there is a fine Flaxman memorial in the church. The house stands in a large wooded park to the right of the photograph. The white mansion visible beyond the bridge is Coombe Park.

Whitchurch Bridge

A long and rather pretty iron toll bridge links Whitchurch and Pangbourne, a late nineteenth-century replacement of the old and rather precarious timber bridge. Despite its apparently rural setting, this bridge leads directly to the heart of Pangbourne. This is now a busy commuter town in which traces of its more exciting past as an Edwardian resort, popular with boaters, anglers and weekenders at the Swan Hotel, can still be detected. Here, the little river Pang joins the Thames, and here Kenneth Grahame, author of *The Wind in the Willows*, spent the last years of his life. However, Pangbourne is probably best known for its Nautical College, which gives the town a distinctly maritime flavour.

This stretch of the river is traditionally popular with anglers, but long gone are the days when Pangbourne was famous for its trout.

Whitchurch

The much rebuilt Norman church of St Mary, with its distinctive wooden spire and good memorial brasses, stands in the centre of Whitchurch, a quiet village with old houses straggling up along the single street that leads away from the river. Beyond it are great acres of beechwoods, bounded far to the north by Goring Heath. Whitchurch's great virtue is its setting, and it is a good starting point for wood and heathland walks. The riverfront is dominated by the old mill, a grand brick building whose colour is echoed throughout the village

In Whitchurch gardens reach down towards the river, a feature of the area, particularly among the grander houses, many of which used to boast riverside boathouses.

Hardwick House

A visiting canal boat, far from its base on the Grand Union Canal north of London, and exploring the Thames perhaps for the first time, drifts past Hardwick House, a handsome brick mansion in the Tudor style. Although much rebuilt, this is at heart still one of the oldest houses in the Thames valley, with clear pre-Tudor origins. Apparently, the estate was established as the family seat of the De Herdewykes at the time of the Norman Conquest. Queen Elizabeth stayed here, and Charles I is reputed to have spent hours playing bowls on the lawn that sweeps down towards the river. For centuries it was owned by the Lybbe family, and it is the diaries of Mrs Lybbe Powys, written at the end of the eighteenth century, that give an interesting picture of the social life of the Thames valley at that time.

The Riverside Boathouse

At one time the banks of the Thames between Oxford and Windsor were dotted with private boathouses, decorative structures either self-contained or in the grounds of grand mansions. Many were built from timber, with extensive use of barge boarding and other ornamental features. This example, near Reading, is a rare survivor of what today is an endangered species. It shows many typical characteristics, for example the balcony over the water, and the living quarters built over the boat garage in which the skiff or the launch could be moored. Many of these boathouses were quite isolated, sometimes with access only from the river, or via a long footpath, but they were, none the less, an essential component of the boating scene in the Edwardian era and between the wars.

Reading

The revival of Reading as a commercial centre is a phenomenon of the late twentieth century, and modern buildings by the Thames underline the town's new found wealth. Beneath these, though, there are layers of history. In the ninth century the marauding Danes made the town an important base, and in the twelfth century a great Benedictine Abbey was founded here. Three hundred years later Reading had become a famous cloth town, with 140 clothiers at work. In the Tudor period parliament sometimes sat here, driven from London by plague; and in the Civil War the town suffered greatly at the hands of Cromwell. The Victorians made the town into a great industrial and agricultural centre, with engineering works and breweries. Their dynamic century also saw the development of the two great businesses long synonymous with Reading but now no more: Huntley & Palmer's biscuits and Sutton's seeds. Behind the modern architecture, Reading is still at heart a Victorian town.

The River Kennet

On a misty winter's day the river is all but invisible, and Duke Street bridge has the mysterious quality of a Whistler painting. The Kennet is one of the major tributaries of the Thames, and their confluence is just to the east of Reading's centre, overlooked by Caversham Park. This is the start of one of England's major inland waterways, the Kennet & Avon Canal, opened in 1810 to link London and Bristol via Reading, Devizes and Bath. Designed by John Rennie, the canal has a number of remarkable engineering features, including the Dundas aqueduct near Bath and the great flight of twenty-nine locks at Caen Hill, near Devizes. After a somewhat chequered existence, the canal fell into decay and closed in the 1950s. Since then, it has been painstakingly restored, section by section, and now boats can once again set out from Reading on a remarkable inland voyage across the heart of England.

Sonning Bridge

An old bridge of soft red brick in the warm sunlight and dappled trees by the riverside capture the spirit of Sonning. This pretty, even picturesque village is at the heart of an attractive and understandably popular stretch of the Thames, which winds its way among islands and in and out of the trees. Sonning appealed greatly to Charles Dickens, who wrote: 'a few minutes' walk inland will disclose as pretty a little place as can well be desired, containing many excellent houses ... and with good old-fashioned gardens.' Near the bridge is the church, remarkable for its collection of brasses and monuments which indicate Sonning's erstwhile importance. In the eleventh century the village was the centre of the diocese of Wiltshire and Berkshire, and until the Reformation the Bishop of Salisbury lived in a grand and sumptuous palace here, of which no trace remains today.

Swans near Sonning

For centuries swans have enjoyed the status of royal birds, and those on the Thames seem always to have been particularly favoured. During the reign of Henry VII, for example, robbers of swans' eggs were condemned to a year in prison and a fine to be determined by the sovereign. The owning and marking of swans has, similarly, long been a royal privilege, and one enjoyed since time immemorial by the Dyers' and Vintners' Companies. Swan-upping, the process of counting and marking the year's cygnets to establish ownership, is an 800-year-old tradition carried out annually in July under the direction of the Queen's Swan Keeper.

Disliked by anglers, feared by small children and sometimes abused by carelessly driven boats, swans are still an essential component of any Thames journey, and they are, quite rightly, still protected.

HENLEY TO LONDON

Henley is the first town that is really on the Thames. The bridge and the fine buildings adjacent to it dominate the river, and the regatta, the town's main claim to fame, underlines the close links between the two. The river's course from Henley is increasingly dramatic and justifiably popular, with long stretches of steep woodland filling the narrow valley and sweeping down to the water. This continues through Medmenham, Hurley, Marlow, Cookham and on towards Maidenhead.

Country houses, some former abbeys, pretty villages and handsome towns reflect the long-established popularity of this region. From Maidenhead, the heart of Thames tourism in the late Victorian and Edwardian eras, the valley and the landscape open out, and the Thames becomes a truly regal river as it approaches Windsor with the famous skyline of the castle high above the water. Between Windsor and Richmond the landscape and the surroundings are more domestic and increasingly suburban but somehow the river maintains its visual appeal and its historical integrity. The Thames here carries the stamp of centuries of history, linking as it does Windsor, Eton, Runnymede and the Magna Carta, Hampton Court, Kingston, Richmond, Kew and Chiswick, places crucial in any appreciation of England's royal, political, imperial and cultural history. Several tributaries enlarge the Thames in this section, the Colne, the Wey and the Mole, and it is a substantial river that winds its way round Hampton Court, Twickenham, Richmond and Chiswick in a series of dramatic bends. At Teddington, the Thames, which has flowed steadily eastwards through Gloucestershire, Oxfordshire, Berkshire, Buckinghamshire, Surrey and Middlesex, meets the influence of the sea, becoming from that point subject to tidal change.

The Henley Royal Regatta

The Season, that outmoded yet still enticing expression of the British social calendar, includes several sporting events in its list of the absolutely essential. These include Royal Ascot, the Derby, Wimbledon, Lord's Test Match and, of course, Henley Royal Regatta. Held early in July, when the weather should be good but can be dreadful, the regatta manages to maintain a balance between the conflicting demands of international sport and the British social scene. The river banks may be lined with corporate hospitality marquees full of the overdressed and the overfed who may not even know one end of an oar from the other, but somehow the Thames and the competitive rowing retain the high ground. For all the nonsense and the frivolity, Henley is, in the eyes of the world, a major sporting occasion.

Henley: the Umpire Starts the Race

A few details apart, this view is probably unchanged since 1839, when the very first Henley Regatta was held. Its origins go back a few years earlier, to 1829, when the first Oxford and Cambridge boat race took place between Hambledon Lock and Henley Bridge. This course was used again in 1837, when the thousands of spectators who lined the banks underlined the enthusiasm that rowing races could generate. The town of Henley raised the money for a Grand Challenge Cup for eights, and since then the regatta has never looked back, growing steadily in diversity, fame and importance ever since. One of the first river regattas, Henley Regatta was given its royal title in 1851. Expanding through the Victorian and Edwardian eras, and acquiring in the process its social aspect, Henley remained none the less an essentially parochial affair, and it is only in this century that it has become a genuinely international occasion.

Henley: the Regatta Course

Since its early days the regatta has used broadly the same course, the long straight Henley Reach from around Temple Island to near the town bridge. There have been variations over the years, mainly designed to make the course as regular and balanced as possible. The races are run along a staked course laid out on a river kept clear of all extraneous craft. Visibility is excellent, allowing spectators on the banks or in boats to see virtually the whole of the course.

Temple Island takes its name from the classical structure that stands on it. This was built as a kind of eye-catcher for Fawley Court, a grand riverside mansion designed in 1771 by James Wyatt. It is also called Regatta Island, having been associated so long with the start of the races. This view shows the island and its temple as a background to an eight driving hard into the current, with the umpire's launch in hot pursuit.

Henley: the Social Scene

The Henley Royal Regatta is a colourful event and has always been so. The 1939 edition of Salter's *Guide to the Thames* describes the scene as: 'vivid with bright dresses, cushions and sunshades, a blaze of rich colour mirrored in the water and set off by the cool greens of the trees and lawns'. Fifty years earlier, Henley was just as popular, but rather more chaotic:

The river is so inconveniently crowded with steam launches, house boats, skiffs, gigs, punts, dingys, canoes, and every other conceivable and inconceivable variety of craft, that the racing boats have sometimes the greatest difficulty in threading a way through the crowd.

Today, the racing is the main event, strictly controlled to international standards, but in the evening there is plenty of time for relaxation.

Henley-on-Thames: the Town

For much of the year Henley is a classic Thames market town, set among wooded hills and enjoying at its heart a grand stone bridge in the eighteenth-century classical style, adorned with heads emblematic of the rivers Thames and Isis, and a fine church whose battlemented tower dominates the town and its surrounding landscape. Hart Street, still flanked by old houses and inns, leads from the bridge to the town centre, and sets the tone. A large town hall, a famous brewery and the delightful Kenton Theatre, built in 1805, add to Henley's appeal, but in the end the main attraction is the river. Developed by the Victorians as a major riverside resort, Henley really came of age with the establishment of the regatta and the arrival of the railway. Since then, the town has never really looked back, remaining throughout the season a boating mecca.

Hambleden

After the long and straight Henley Reach the river enters the sweeping bend that carries it round Remenham Hill and into a more dramatic landscape of attractively wooded hills. Greenlands, an Italianate house whose lawns reach down to the water's edge, has an exciting history. Now a college, the house was owned by the Royalist Doyley family during the Civil War and survived a long siege by Cromwell's forces before finally surrendering. Completely rebuilt in the 1850s, it then became the home of the Right Honourable W. H. Smith, whose career started with railway bookstalls and finished as First Lord of the Treasury. From Greenlands there is a view along the river to the next lock, Hambleden, where the large weir is overlooked by the delightful weatherboarded mill.

Hambleden Mill

There has been a mill at Hambleden at least since the Domesday Book and the present building can trace its origins back to the sixteenth century. Built on a grand scale and with the kind of natural elegance that is characteristic of many early industrial buildings, Hambleden is a classic mill, and a rare survivor. So many Thames mills have been swept away, often for no good reason. Inevitably this is no longer a working mill, having been converted into flats, but it has been done sympathetically, retaining so many of the essential vernacular details, and so it is still a marvellous riverside scene. From Hambleden the Thames Path follows the river's winding course to Medmenham, where the former abbey was infamous in the late eighteenth century as the setting for the orgiastic activities of Sir Francis Dashwood's Hell Fire Club, whose members lived up to its motto: *Fay ce que voudras* ('Do whatever you want').

Temple Lock

After Medmenham, there are two locks close together. The first, at Hurley, is a pretty spot where the river breaks into several water courses, creating a series of islands. The village of Hurley is away to the south, half hidden by trees. Here was yet another priory, on a site traditionally the burial place of the sister of Edward the Confessor, and associated with Westminster Abbey. Little remains to be seen, but apparently Henry VIII gave Hurley Wood to Westminster Abbey in exchange for Covent Garden. The second lock, Temple, is also attractive, with flowery gardens, generous lawns and well-cut topiary. Another great Thames mill stood here, famous at least since the eighteenth century for the making of paper. The Temple name comes from the Knights Templar, long connected with the part of the river through Bisham Abbey, founded by them as a preceptory in the twelfth century.

Bisham Abbey

Bisham Abbey is well known today as a National Sports Centre. Owned by the English Sports Council, its training facilities and grounds are used by footballers, athletes, tennis players and many others in training for national squads or under the direction of their respective governing bodies. This modern role has rather overshadowed the Abbey's important history, first as a Preceptory for the Knights Templar and then as an Augustine priory and one of the major religious buildings of the Thames valley. After the dissolution of the monasteries, Bisham became a house, to be presented by Henry VIII to his rejected wife, Anne of Cleves. She passed it over to the Hoby family, who sheltered the future Queen Elizabeth here. For centuries it was a classic English mansion, complete with ghost. The adjacent church, which was never associated directly with the abbey, contains wonderful figured Hoby tombs.

Marlow from Winter Hill

Cutting its way through the Chilterns, the Thames has, for miles, been flanked by great beech woods. These rise to a climax at Winter Hill, a dominant feature on the south bank whose open top is now in the care of the National Trust, with unrivalled views of the river's winding course past Marlow, Bourne End and Cookham, and over the whole Thames valley from Henley to Maidenhead. Charles Dickens described this as 'a view as magnificent as it is extensive.' New roads, notably the M4, the M40 and their links, which include the new Thames bridge shown here, have encouraged extensive development in this area. However, the all-encompassing woodlands have managed to absorb the impact of these changes, and keep alive the area's particular appeal. A walk from the river up through Quarry Wood and out on to the bare heights of Winter Hill is still as enjoyable as ever.

Marlow

The prettiest suspension bridge on the river, designed by Tierny Clark in 1835, and Gilbert Scott's flint and stone Holy Trinity church, completed in 1852, give Marlow a decidedly nineteenth-century look. This is deceptive, for at heart Marlow is an eighteenth-century market town and riverside resort, with plenty of fine buildings in the picturesque St Peter's Street and the wide High Street. Continuing popularity has brought extensive modern development, without destroying the town's essential appeal, which has drawn many famous residents, for example the Shelleys in 1817-18; Mary Shelley wrote *Frankenstein* in their cottage here. Other Marlow writers include Thomas Peacock and T. S. Eliot.

Despite its many attractions, Marlow is seen at its best by the Thames. The lock is in a lovely setting, by the crashing weir just below the bridge. Across the river the famous Compleat Angler inn and restaurant underlines the area's lasting appeal to fishermen.

Cookham

Commuting, retirement and their associated leisure activities have made their mark on the Thames in both Buckinghamshire and Berkshire, but somehow the riverside towns and villages retain their traditional character. They are often saved by the unalterable nature of the landscape of the wooded valley, at its best around Cookham and Cliveden. Cookham, initially attractive, is less so as it spreads inland from the bridge, made famous by the village's most famous resident, Sir Stanley Spencer. Cookham views occur in many Spencer paintings and there is an exhibition devoted to this local celebrity in the King's Hall. Another local artist, Frederick Walker, is commemorated in the church. Across the river are the dense woods that rise steeply to hide Hedsor church and Hedsor House, a Victorian mansion whose tower can be seen above the trees.

Cliveden

Below Cookham the river divides to form Formosa Island, and from here the magnificent Cliveden woods run unbroken to Maidenhead. Rising above the woods, high above the river, is Cliveden, perhaps the most famous house in the Thames valley. Now owned by the National Trust, and in a new reincarnation as a grand hotel, the house was designed by Sir Charles Barry for the Duke of Sutherland and completed in 1862. Wonderful gardens surround the Italianate mansion. Later owned by the Duke of Westminster, it passed in 1893 to the Astors. From that point Cliveden became synonymous with political intrigue, artistic life and social scandals, a pattern of events culminating with the Profumo affair of the early 1960s. Several houses preceded the present Cliveden. The first was built in 1679 for Charles Villiers, the notorious Duke of Buckingham. It was here that he brought the Countess of Shrewsbury, after killing her husband in a duel.

Boulter's Lock

Traditionally, one of the most popular locks on the Thames is Boulter's, near Maidenhead. In the Edwardian era, and into the interwar years, Maidenhead was a fashionable riverside resort. It was particularly popular with weekend visitors who stayed at the smart Skindles Hotel and made leisurely explorations of the river by boat. As a result, Boulter's Lock was always busy, and there are many photographs, and a famous painting by Gregory, showing it packed with every type of craft. Some years ago, this scene was recreated. Here, one of the participating punts, suitably decorated, makes its way to the lock.

As a town, Maidenhead has no outstanding charms, but its popularity was well known to Dickens, who wrote in 1888:

Whether for the angler, the artist, the oarsman, or the simple tourist; whether for picnicking and, it has even been whispered "spooning", to say nothing of camping out, there are few places in England to beat the Cliveden Reach at Maidenhead.

Ray Mill

The growth of Maidenhead has always been inspired by transport. Initially the river encouraged the building of medieval wharfs and a bridge. In the eighteenth century turnpikes brought coaching inns and some domestic development of the London side of the town. However, it was with the coming of the railway that Maidenhead really took off, and its expansion into a riverside resort in the late nineteenth century was railway-driven. The emergence of pleasure boating as a popular pastime turned the emphasis back on to the river, and brought extensive building of villas and cottages along the bank and around the hitherto rather secluded Ray Mill area. With Boulter's Lock, which was completely rebuilt in 1912, becoming a boating centre, the adjacent Ray Mill island was turned into a public pleasure garden. With the coming of the car and its gradual dominance, Maidenhead changed from a resort into a modern commuter suburb, but lingering echoes of the Edwardian resort can still be found.

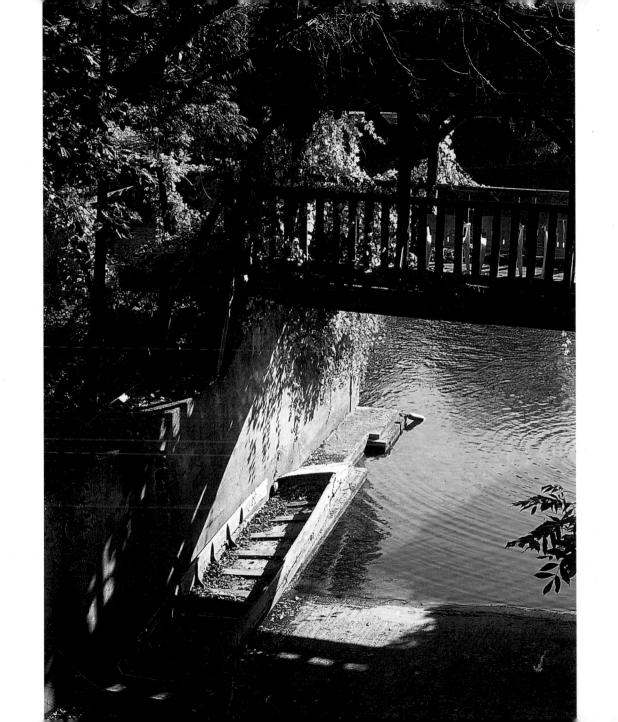

Maidenhead Floods

During the winter and spring the Thames regularly overflows its banks, a necessary reminder of the massive, fast-flowing river that lurks beneath the placid stream enjoyed by summer boaters. Flood scenes such as this, to the west of Maidenhead bridge, are by no means uncommon, making the towpath impassable and frequently stranding carelessly parked cars whose owners had overlooked the speed with which the waters can rise. The Thames is a river for all seasons. The delights of summer are obvious, and equally attractive are spring flowers and autumn leaves, especially where beech woods line the banks. The Thames in winter is more of an acquired taste, but the power of the water rushing through a monochrome landscape of bare trees, beneath a leaden sky, can also be exciting.

Maidenhead Bridges

Maidenhead's bridges are its best feature. Each is a masterpiece and yet their styles, artistic symmetry and engineering bravura, could not be more different. Sir Robert Taylor's road bridge was built in 1772, a beautifully balanced series of classical arches in well-cut stone and topped by a handsome balustrade, one of the best of the river's eighteenth-century bridges. Isambard Kingdom Brunel's rail bridge, designed for his beloved Great Western Railway, was built in brick with two graceful arches, which, at 123 feet, are still the longest and the flattest brick arches in the world. At its completion in 1839 it was a wonder of the modern world, and a resounding defeat for his many detractors who said it had to collapse. Turner's great painting, 'Rain, Steam and Speed', shows a train crossing this bridge.

Towards Windsor

At Maidenhead the Thames goes
through one of its complete
changes. Gone are the steep
banks, the flanking hills and the
glorious beech woods as the river
flows into a far more suburban
landscape, dominated by the
modern developments of the M4
corridor. There are, however,
some high points, for example
the medieval timber-framed
Ockwells Manor; the Tudor
brickwork of Dorney Court
where England's first pineapple
was grown; eighteenth-century
Down Place with its literary
association through the Kit Kat
Club, the curious eighteenth-
century French *singerie* paintings
that gave the name to Monkey
Island; and the sadly disused but
delightfully remote riverside
church at Boveney. However, all
these are put in the shade by the
great towering bulk of Windsor
Castle, which fills the horizon
throughout the otherwise dull
landscape beneath the Heathrow
flightpath.

Windsor Castle

Without doubt the most familiar
skyline in Britain, Windsor has
dominated the Thames for
centuries. Impressive, enduring
and massively built over
centuries, Windsor seems the
perfect royal palace. At its heart
is Edward III's great round tower,
sitting on top of a natural
stronghold that has been a
fortress since pre-Roman times. A
royal residence since William the
Conqueror, Windsor bears the
mark of almost every monarch,
with major contributions having
been made by Henry I, Henry III,
Edward I, Edward III, Henry VII,
Charles II, and later by George
IV and Queen Victoria. The
inspired restoration that followed
the recent fire has added the
present Queen to this list. The
result is a fairy palace,
wonderfully sited above the river,
and offering from its towers
remarkable views over the town
and the surrounding parks.

Eton College

The compact town of Eton, little more than the High Street, is separated from Windsor only by the river, and a bridge ties the two together. Visually, they are part of the same broad view. As a town, Eton is, of course, subservient to its college. Founded in 1440 by Henry VI, Eton is Britain's best known public school. Adjacent to Windsor Castle and linked by the Thames to both the University of Oxford and the Palace of Westminster, its position reflects its place in English history and society. Overlooking one of the river's great sweeping bends, Eton's buildings add further magic to that already engendered by Windsor Castle. Most significant is the fifteenth-century chapel with its high pinnacled roof dominating a skyline of towers and battlements, a building designed by Henry to be larger than many cathedrals.

Romney Lock

The best way to see Windsor and Eton is from a boat on the river, pausing in Romney Lock to enjoy the views of Eton College. Second best is from the towpath. A walk from Boveney Lock is full of delights, passing Windsor race course and enjoying the constantly changing patterns of the towers of Windsor Castle as the river twists and turns. The path goes under the railway bridge carrying the former Great Western line from Paddington, the first to reach Windsor and the one used frequently by Queen Victoria. It then follows the curving river along the Windsor quayside, past Eton and on to Romney Lock, with views of the College chapel. Romney Lock, its building rather like a discreet 1920s petrol station, looks out on to the great expanse of Windsor's Home Park. Then comes Black Potts Bridge, carrying the rival South Western line from Waterloo, and the Victoria road bridge. Walking the other way is just as enjoyable too.

Near Runnymede

There was a Saxon palace in Old
Windsor and it remained a Royal
residence until 1110, when
Henry I moved the court to
Windsor Castle. Nothing remains
today, but among the bungalows
and modern estates there is still a
priory and a thirteenth-century
church. Old Windsor was the
setting for a curious piece of
Royal patronage, the setting up in
the late 1870s of the Royal
Tapestry Works. This example of
Victorian enterprise was destined
never to be a rival to Aubusson
or even Mortlake.

From here suburban life
encroaches steadily, but somehow
the spirit of the river survives as
it makes its way past Wraysbury
and Egham, and on towards
Staines. Staines was once a
pleasant market town, and
despite modern development a
bit of that old atmosphere
survives around the bridge, a
handsome early nineteenth-
century structure by John Rennie.
Near the bridge, and protected by
iron railings, is the London Stone,
marking the former limit of the
jurisdiction of the Corporation of
London over the river.

Runnymede

The last oasis of peace and quiet
on the river's route to London is
Runnymede, a large expanse of
parkland backed by the slopes of
Cooper's Hill. Here, on an island
in the Thames, King John was
compelled to sign the Magna
Carta in 1215, a moment that
marks the beginning of modern
English history, the symbolic
establishment of freedom
guaranteed by law. As a
celebration of this, Runnymede,
now in the care of the National
Trust, is the setting for a series of
memorials. There is the
restrained classicism of the
Magna Carta memorial itself;
nearby is the Kennedy memorial
on an acre of ground given in
perpetuity to the American
people; and high above on the
hill there is the Commonwealth
Air Forces memorial, an elegantly
modern structure designed by Sir
Edward Maufe, the architect of
Guildford cathedral.

Houseboats near Hampton

In a landscape of great reservoirs, the Thames twists and turns past Weybridge and the Wey Navigation to Guildford and Godalming, and via the Wey to the Basingstoke Canal, past Shepperton and Walton-on-Thames, a town remarkable for its lack of interest in the river. The meandering course provides plenty of backwaters where houseboats of every imaginable form have traditionally rested. It is a long established tradition in Britain to live afloat, often in rather surprising ways and, while the rich diversity of domesticized craft on the rivers and canals before the war and into the 1950s is now much reduced, there are still good ones to be found. Here are two extreme examples: the modern suburban house lifted bodily on to a pontoon, granting nothing to maritime tradition, and the older type of converted naval vessel, a rare survivor from the fleets of retired motor torpedo boats, Fairmile launches and naval pinnaces that used to litter the waterways.

Garrick's Temple

Approaching London, the Middlesex or northern shore of the Thames is generally more attractive than the Surrey shore. This is particularly true of the Hampton area, where a group of handsome buildings surround a decorative early nineteenth-century church, well placed among trees on the riverside. Molesey, on the Surrey side, is by comparison a featureless sprawl of suburban housing. Hampton's popularity is well established, the actor David Garrick having come to live here in 1754, in a house subsequently redeveloped by Adam. The gardens ran down to the river, and here Garrick had a classical temple erected to house a bust of Shakespeare by the sculptor Roubiliac. The elegance of the eighteenth century is strong in Hampton, but it is balanced by the eccentric frivolity of the nearby Swiss chalet that houses Huck's boatyard. In the Thames is Taggs Island, now residential, but rather more racy in the 1920s and 1930s when it was known as Thames Riviera and Palm Beach.

Hampton Court Palace

In 1514 Cardinal Wolsey acquired some land at Hampton and started work on what he intended to be the largest and grandest private house in England. In the process he offended his king, Henry VIII, who compelled Wolsey to hand over the unfinished house as a gift in 1526. Under Henry's guidance the house was completed in great style and at enormous cost, becoming his favourite royal palace. Other monarchs both favoured and added to Hampton Court and it remained a royal residence until the time of George II. Much English history has taken place within the palace, for example the marriage of Henry VIII and Katherine Parr, the second trial of Mary Queen of Scots and the decision to produce the authorized version of the Bible. Many architects made a contribution, notably Wren, who was responsible for this Thames-facing facade, part of a major section containing the State Rooms and surrounding the Fountain Court.

The Gardens at Hampton Court

Several monarchs greatly enjoyed Hampton Court, notably Henry VIII, Queen Elizabeth and Charles I. However, the greatest contribution to the house was probably made by William and Mary, for whom it was virtually a permanent home. They expanded the house and its contents, but as great a legacy of their time is Hampton Court's surrounding garden and park. Following contemporary European, and particularly Dutch, traditions, they created one of England's finest formal gardens. This reflected the style of the house and the open courts around which it was built, contrasting deliberately with the huge expanse of natural parkland to the north, and separating it clearly from the Thames. All the glories of the formal garden were there, including a maze and magnificent wrought ironwork. In later centuries much of William and Mary's garden disappeared, but ambitious restoration projects are now under way.

Kingston

Kingston's name reveals its history as a former royal borough where seven Saxon kings were crowned, on a stone displayed outside the Guildhall. Modern Kingston is a busy shopping centre at the heart of surrounding suburbia, but the old market place still retains a sense of a more interesting past. The town is at its best by the river, a pleasant and generous area dominated by the early nineteenth-century stone bridge. Its predecessor, a timber structure, was apparently the setting in April 1745 for one of the last recorded uses of the ducking stool in England, when a local lady innkeeper was ducked for scolding, in the presence of over two thousand people. The converted barge in the foreground, with its floating 'garden' is another variation on the theme of the Thames houseboat.

Teddington

At Teddington the Thames in effect comes of age and meets the sea. The great complex of locks and weirs here mark the boundary between the non-tidal and tidal sections of the river. There are several locks, ranging from the 49-foot skiff lock to the massive 650-foot barge lock. It is an exciting place, busy in summer with all kinds of traffic, and dramatic in winter with the weirs in full flow. It is also popular with fishermen, pursuing the perch, roach, dace, carp, tench, barbel, gudgeon, pike, trout, eel, bream, chub, pope and minnows that are regular inhabitants of the non-tidal waters. The official boundary that denotes the start of the jurisdiction of the Port of London Authority, responsible for the tideway since 1909, is marked by an obelisk 265 yards below Teddington Lock. The body responsible for the non-tidal Thames is constantly changing: from 1857 it was the Thames Conservancy, then the National Rivers Authority and now it is the Environment Agency.

Richmond

Spreading over a hillside above the bridge and overlooking the Thames, Richmond has somehow retained the atmosphere of an eighteenth-century resort, a feeling deliberately exploited by the architect Quinlan Terry's neo-Georgian riverside development by the bridge, completed in 1988. Despite its historical style, the modern town overlays much earlier history, for Richmond, or Sheen as it was then known, was the setting for two royal palaces that were in use for five centuries, from Edward I to Charles I. Nothing remains today except the gateway. It was Charles who first enclosed and stocked the 2,000-acre Great Park, which remains one of the finest of the royal parks. Public access is guaranteed by the famous lawsuit of 1758, when George II failed in his attempt to exclude the public. Many well-known people have lived in Richmond, not least the actor Edmund Kean, who is buried in the church.

Richmond Hill

The view of the river from Richmond Hill is justly famous and is the subject of numerous paintings by artists as varied as Wilson and Steer. Charles Dickens was captivated by it, writing in 1888: 'Nothing in the neighbourhood of London is better known or more delightful than the view from Richmond Hill', and when Sir Walter Scott described it as 'an unrivalled landscape', he was hardly saying too much.

The Thames sweeps round the hill in a broad curve and the trees that cover the banks effectively hide all the modern riverside developments, and retain the illusion of the landscape being some great eighteenth-century park by Capability Brown, or bringing to life some eighteenth-century Italianate painting. It is a magical spot, especially in the soft light of evening, or early morning.

Marble Hill House

A sequence of grand houses flank the Thames as it winds its way towards London. First is Ham House, set back from the river, and in its architecture and contents the complete expression of seventeenth-century taste. A complete contrast is Strawberry Hill, near Twickenham, Walpole's eccentric but pioneering mid-eighteenth-century essay in the Gothic revival, designed for him by Chute and Bentley to house his extraordinary collection. Nearby are more conventional expressions of eighteenth-century style. York House, and even better, Marble Hill House, are pure Palladian classicism and the perfect foil to Walpole's spiky pinnacles. Beautifully restored, this delightful miniature mansion was built by George II for his mistress, Henrietta Howard. Set in a park that sweeps down to the river, it looks like a doll's house in its perfect symmetry and soft colours.

Kew

Two more grand houses, Richmond Lodge, Kew Palace and their parks, formed the basis for the Royal Botanical Gardens at Kew, dating from 1841. The gardens, adjacent to Richmond Park, and filling the southern bank of the long Syon Reach, are full of curiosities, not always of a botanical nature. One of the most unexpected is the Chinese pagoda, designed by Sir William Chambers in the eighteenth century to decorate the gardens of Kew Palace. Kew itself is still at heart a riverside village formed around a green, facing the entrance to the Botanical Gardens. Buried in the early eighteenth-century church are the painters Gainsborough and Zoffany, underlining the broad appeal of this part of Thames-side London to smart society in their lifetime.

LONDON

From Richmond the Thames becomes an increasingly urban river, built up on both banks and carrying the impact of centuries of development. At Hammersmith the suburbs disappear, along with the last vestiges of the river's rural roots. The big tidal flow alternately fills the river and exposes a large expanse of muddy foreshore, cleaning and aerating the city as it comes and goes. The first of the real London bridges is Hammersmith, a suitably ornate affair rather like the last, Tower Bridge. In between, eighteen others keep London moving, not to mention the various road and rail tunnels. Initially houses and factories flank the river, with rather more of the latter on the southern shore, and in between are parks and green spaces, all visibly telling the history of London since the seventeenth century. Bishop's palaces and churches great and small maintain those Christian links established with the river in the eleventh century and in their variety tell the story of London's religious life. Embankments contain and control the river, and add promenades and riverside thoroughfares, necessities of city life. Power stations, railway stations, old quays and docks and commercial buildings of all kinds add to the interest and then, at London's heart, the Palace of Westminster and Westminster Abbey stand together, church and state united by the Thames.

Next comes the old city, with modern buildings surrounding St Paul's and the Tower of London. Then, after the triumphal gateway that Tower Bridge represents, the Thames sweeps in broad bends through London's new city, the regenerated Docklands, to Greenwich, still the grandest architectural vista on the river. From Greenwich industries old and new dominate the banks of a broad river widened still further by the waters of the Lea as the Thames sweeps on the Barrier, technical wizardry by man to control the river's wilder impulses.

Feeding the Birds at Hammersmith

The Thames enters London in a series of great loops that carries it past Brentford (where the Grand Union Canal joins the river), Mortlake, Chiswick and Hammersmith. In the process it finally separates itself from those lingering rural associations that have marked its last few miles, to become an urban waterway. Fine houses still mark the banks: Syon, Chiswick, Osterley and the impact of the eighteenth century can still be enjoyed in riverside terraces in Chiswick and Hammersmith. However, the classicism is now definitely urban, a formal accompaniment for a river whose tidal flow exposes great areas of foreshore. Here, at low tide, it is feeding time for the swans, gulls, geese and pigeons that are a permanent part of London's river.

Hammersmith Bridge

London's bridges are richly diverse, reflecting all the architectural styles and structural techniques popular in the nineteenth and twentieth centuries. Bridges have crossed the Thames since at least the Middle Ages and several eighteenth-century ones lingered on until they were swept away on a tide of Victorian progress. Equally, many of the bridges constructed by the Victorians were new river crossings, reflecting the enormous growth in traffic. Typical of these is the delightfully ornate suspension bridge at Hammersmith, built in 1887 to the designs of Sir Joseph Bazalgette. Recent repainting has highlighted the decorative detail which has a distinctive French feel, particularly in the entertaining little pavilion roofs that top the towers. Since its closure to most traffic, the bridge's fine views along the river banks can now be enjoyed in relative peace.

Rowing at Putney

Putney has, for decades, been London's rowing centre. The growth of the sport was greatly encouraged by the popularity of the Oxford and Cambridge boat race, which was first rowed over the Putney to Mortlake course in 1845. Since then, the boathouses of schools and rowing clubs have spread westwards along the south bank from Putney Bridge. This, a grand structure opened in 1886, replaced an early eighteenth-century wooden toll bridge. A walk along the embankment road that separates the boathouses from the river can be full of interest, with eights, fours, sculls and other craft filling the tideway and the sloping shore. Across the river is Fulham Palace, now the main residence of the Bishop of London, but formerly one of his country seats. Parts of the palace are sixteenth century but most of the buildings are newer. The palace's occasionally rowdy neighbour is Fulham Football Club.

Albert Bridge

The Thames' Chelsea Reach, flanked to the south by the trees of Battersea Park, is framed by two suspension bridges. The more decorative of the two is the Albert Bridge, a spiky and vaguely Gothic structure designed by W. Ordish and opened in 1873. By day, the lightness of the colour scheme emphasizes its frivolous delicacy, while by night its array of twinkling lights gives it a magical quality. Marching troops are still instructed to break step when crossing. Chelsea Bridge, its partner, is more utilitarian, reflecting its recent date. On the north, the river has a fine promenade in the form of the embankment, completed between Chelsea Bridge and Battersea Bridge in 1874, from which there are excellent views of the buildings and gardens of the Royal Hospital. On the south, the mud and shingle foreshore revealed at low tide is a reminder of the river's appearance before the Victorians built the embankments.

Chelsea Housing

The elegant eighteenth-century terraces that flank the river at Hammersmith return again at Chelsea, but rather blighted now by the main road that separates them from the river. Originally they would have enjoyed riverside gardens and a more peaceful aspect. Nevertheless, these houses have always been popular, with notable artistic and literary associations. Rising above their classic façades and the well-defined London roofscape of the early nineteenth century is the late twentieth-century answer to urban living. More unexpected perhaps are the houseboats ranged along the shoreline. This collection of converted barges, pontoons and other craft have long been associated with this part of the river, and represent one of London's major colonies of water dwellers. Featured in many films, their fittings range from the spartan to the extremely luxurious.

Battersea Park

Battersea Park was laid out in 1858, turning a large area of fields into formal gardens complete with paths, vistas, a lake, flower displays and specimen trees. It was here, in 1829, that the Duke of Wellington fought a duel. The park really came into its own in 1951 when, as part of the Festival of Britain, it became the Festival Pleasure Gardens, with restaurants, bars, a theatre, concert pavilion and a huge fun fair, with regular riverboat services from the pier. This entertainment complex soon lost its way but lingered on for many years in one form or another and Battersea is still one of London's most enjoyable parks. A recent feature, which dominates the Battersea riverfront, is the rather extraordinary and richly decorative Peace Pagoda, an enjoyable addition to London's riverside and a fitting complement to other Thames exotica, such as a Swiss chalet and an Egyptian obelisk.

Vauxhall

Parallel to Chelsea Bridge is the broad expanse of the Grosvenor Bridge, opened in 1859 to serve the Victorian railway stations and at that time the widest railway bridge in the world. Since then, it has been widened and rebuilt three times. From here, the Thames curves into the Nine Elms Reach past Pimlico and Vauxhall. Vauxhall Bridge, opened in its present form in 1906, leads to a part of London on the south bank long associated with piecemeal industrial development. For example, this was in the eighteenth century a centre of pottery making. For years run down, and visually unexciting, the Vauxhall riverbank has recently been brought to life in a dramatic manner by the huge and colourful building that houses the headquarters of the security services. A blend of 1930s Art Deco and American-inspired Post-Modernism, this decorative structure looks exciting by both day and night, and throws into high relief the tawdriness of most of the buildings that line the south bank.

The Embankments

A major enterprise in the middle of the nineteenth century was the building of the Thames embankments, under the direction of Sir Joseph Bazalgette. Built over the formerly tidal foreshore, these narrowed the river and speeded its rate of flow, enabling it to become a more efficient remover of the increasing tons of rubbish thrown into it. At the same time, the embankments allowed for the building of riverside roads and walkways raised above, and effectively concealed the huge pipes that carried the newly created sewage services and water mains. Often backed by gardens and sculpture parks, the embankments added a new lease of life to the riverside. The appeal of the broad riverside promenades thus created was greatly increased by the use of decorative cast iron gas lamps and benches. The latter were made in a number of forms and styles, but the more eccentric were those with sphinx or camel supports, designed perhaps to echo then currently popular Egyptian themes.

Battersea from Vauxhall Bridge

In the colours almost of a nocturne by James McNeil Whistler, the greatest of the Victorian painters of the Thames, and with the random shapes of the buildings on the south bank forming a black pattern against the sky, the broad river has a magical quality. In the distance are the old gasometers and the four towering chimneys of Battersea power station. Long disused and partially derelict, this Art Deco masterpiece by Giles Gilbert Scott still dominates the southern riverbank while it awaits its future as a leisure centre. Moored boats are reminders of earlier, busier times when the Thames was a major thoroughfare. There is little traffic on the river today, apart from the regular trains of container barges carting away London's rubbish, and the occasional pleasure boat travelling westwards with the tide.

Millbank

From Battersea to Lambeth the Thames' southern bank is a muddle of indifferent and featureless modern buildings, wasting the great potential offered by a mighty urban riverfront. The northern bank is a complete contrast. Housing developments of differing styles and periods add interest between Chelsea and Pimlico and trees shade the riverside promenade. From Vauxhall Bridge a series of great buildings make their mark: first the Tate Gallery with its grand classical portico in the late Victorian Imperial style; then comes the mighty Millbank Tower, 387 feet of reflective glass and one of the best of London's early towerblocks, dating from 1963; finally the powerful and majestic Art Deco offices built in the 1920s for ICI, with their array of symbolic sculpture by C. S. Jagger, overshadow Lambeth Bridge and pave the way for the Victoria Embankment Gardens and the Palace of Westminster.

The Tate Gallery

London's riverfront by night is always exciting, with the floodlights throwing key buildings into high relief. Typical is the lighting of the Tate Gallery, picking out the classical details of the facade, and giving the dome an eerie quality against the night sky. The building was commissioned by Sir Henry Tate, the great sugar magnate, designed by Sydney R. J. Smith and opened in 1897. Its collections, based on sixty-five paintings donated by Tate, concentrated initially on British art, but were later broadened to include works by nineteenth- and twentieth-century European and American artists. The Tate's links with the river will be underlined by its new annexe, being developed in the former Bankside power station in Southwark, another stylish Art Deco riverside building designed originally by Giles Gilbert Scott.

Charing Cross

Radical changes were made to London's river by Victorian railway companies. Eleven new bridges were built between Kingston and Southwark, but even more striking were the various railway termini. Victoria, Waterloo, Charing Cross, Blackfriars, London Bridge and Cannon Street were all built on sites beside or near the river. Closest to the water is probably Charing Cross, built in 1864 at the end of the iron girders of the Hungerford Bridge. Originally the station had a huge iron and glass trainshed roof, curving a 100 feet above the platforms, but this was replaced after a partial collapse in 1905. Echoes of this great arched roof were incorporated into the nine-storey office block raised over the station in the 1980s. Designed by Terry Farrell, this Post Modern structure combines American-inspired details with the great shapes of the railway age.

The South Bank

In 1951 the Festival of Britain brought to life a stretch of the riverbank formerly the province of small-scale industry. The lasting legacy of this great and popular event was the Festival Hall, now the centre of the South Bank arts complex which includes the Queen Elizabeth Hall, the Hayward Gallery, the National Film Theatre and, right by the river, the National Theatre. This block-like and rather brutalist concrete structure is a powerful reflection of the architectural styles of the 1960s, but it and its surrounding buildings certainly add more to the riverscape than the monolithic towers of the former Shell Centre on the western side of Waterloo Bridge. Along the riverfront is a broad and generous promenade decorated with sculpture, and an excellent place to enjoy the river by day and by night.

The Albert Embankment

Designed as a broad riverside promenade on the south bank, the Albert Embankment connects Lambeth and Westminster bridges. Close by Lambeth bridge is the old Lambeth parish church, now a museum of garden history, and Lambeth Palace, the residence since the twelfth century of the Archbishop of Canterbury. The promenade now passes in front of St Thomas's Hospital, built originally in the 1860s as seven separate but identical Italianate brick blocks, but now extensively reconstructed as one of the most modern hospitals in London. The promenade offers fine views across the river to the Victoria Embankment Gardens, where Rodin's 'Burghers of Calais' sculpture can be seen among the trees, to the Palace of Westminster and to the tall arches of Westminster Bridge, not a particularly elegant structure but one from which there are magnificent panoramas of the river.

The Palace of Westminster

The most familiar and still the greatest architectural view on the Thames in central London is the riverfront of the Palace of Westminster, a long horizontal display of symmetry in pale stone framed by the verticals of the Victoria Tower and Big Ben. The destruction by fire in 1834 of the medieval Houses of Parliament made possible the creation of some marvellous architecture, and Charles Barry rose to the challenge, greatly aided by his assistant, the young Augustus Welby Northmore Pugin. The building is Barry's, but the decoration and fittings belong to Pugin. Completed in 1852, the Palace is in every way a landmark structure. At the time the greatest architectural and interior design scheme in the world, it established Gothic as the style of State in Britain and launched the Gothic Revival on to the western world. It also redefined in its layout and working the British constitution, that is to say the relationship between monarchy, church and state.

FORGET SIX COUNTIES OVERHUNG
                         WITH SMOKE,
FORGET THE SNORTING STEAM AND
                         PISTON STROKE,
FORGET THE SPREADING OF THE
                         HIDEOUS TOWN;
THINK RATHER OF THE PACKHORSE
                         OF THE DOWN,
AND DREAM OF LONDON, SMALL WHITE
                         AND CLEAN,
THE CLEAR THAMES BORDERED BY
                         ITS GARDENS GREEN;

FROM AN EARTHLY PARADISE.
                    WILLIAM MORRIS

Thames-side Poets

At the southern end of Westminster Bridge there is a large lion, set on a plinth on the pavement in 1966. Dating from 1837 and made of Coade Stone, a ceramic form of artificial stone developed in the late eighteenth century, this stood originally on the roof of the long-demolished buildings of the Lion brewery. Adjacent to it is County Hall, a massive stone building in a refined 1920s classicism, formerly the administrative headquarters for London. The embankment promenade continues from here towards Waterloo and the South Bank. Set into the pavement in this section are carved quotations from poems relevant to London, including these lines from William Morris' *Earthly Paradise*. This early display of street art paves the way for the large variety of sculpture on show on and around the promenade as it passes through the South Bank arts complex.

South Bank Sports

Sometimes in the summer the Thames comes to life in unexpected ways. Against the backdrop of Cleopatra's Needle, the bulky Shell building with the largest clock in London, and the more decorative façade of the Savoy Hotel, the river teems with life and activity. A pleasure boat, a tug hauling laden barges, a tiny speed boat and even a small liner seem to be breasting the waves. The liner, called, confusingly, the *Queen Mary*, is actually moored permanently to the shore. This retired Glasgow passenger vessel, built in the 1930s, is now a floating restaurant and bar, one of several on London's river. In the foreground, below the Royal Festival Hall, the low tide seems to have exposed not the usual expanse of dirty mud but a sandy beach. Young canoeists make the most of this rare treat, an indication that the much improved water quality is slowly reviving the river as a vital resource for pleasure and recreation.

From Waterloo Bridge

Waterloo Bridge spans the Thames as it curves round into King's Reach, offering unrivalled panoramas in both directions. This view looks eastwards towards Blackfriars along a quiet river, with moored pleasure boats awaiting the next tourist rush. In stormy light the famous skyline looks its best, and shows to perfection the rich diversity of London's architecture. The tall towers on the left, flanking a seventeenth-century Hawksmoor spire, belong to the Barbican. Modern architecture also dominates the next group, with Sir Richard Rogers' famous Lloyds Building just visible in front of the Commercial Union Tower, a 1960s contribution to the skyline. Still dominant and all conquering despite the assaults of post-war modernism is the wonderful dome of St Paul's, and finally there is the 600-foot National Westminster Tower, still the City's tallest building by far.

From Waterloo Bridge

In the soft evening light the buildings lose their detail, becoming shapes against the sky, and Victorian Gothic Whitehall Court turns into a fairy castle. The street lights are coming on and there are flashes of light from the electric trains. River traffic has stopped and the Festival Pier pontoon has dropped with the low tide. Behind, and cutting across the gentle outline of the trees on the embankment, are the rigid girders of the Hungerford rail bridge and its attached foot bridge, an ungainly 1860s replacement for the earlier suspension bridge but still an essential London landmark. Beyond are moored restaurant and bar boats, notably the *Tattershall Castle*, a retired paddle steamer that spent its working life ploughing to and fro across the Humber.

Egyptian London

London is full of unexpected exotica, strange reflections of past enthusiasms and fashions. In the late nineteenth century the Victorians were fascinated by Egypt and the Middle East, a passion encouraged by excavated discoveries from ancient Egypt and by the increasing ease of travel. As a result, many buildings of this period have Egyptian-inspired decorative details. Linked to this was the fashion for Islamic styles, reflected by the many colourful tiled interiors created at this time. Even the original 1870 underground station at Blackfriars was in the Turkish style, complete with minarets. The Egyptian collections at the British Museum probably inspired the sculptor George Vulliamy when he modelled the pair of bronze sphinxes that stand guard at the base of Cleopatra's Needle. Across the road is another less exotic but still foreign contribution to London's history, the Belgian war memorial of 1920, with sinuous sculptures by Victor Rousseau.

Cleopatra's Needle

Despite its name, this Egyptian obelisk originally erected at Heliopolis in about 1500BC by Thothmes III, has nothing to do with Cleopatra. One of a pair (the other is in New York), it was given to Britain in 1819 and finally put up by the Thames in 1878, after an adventurous journey which included it being cast adrift and abandoned in a storm in the Bay of Biscay. Over 68 feet high and weighing 180 tons, the obelisk stands on top of a time capsule, containing among other things a portrait of Queen Victoria, a box of hairpins, copies of Bradshaw's *Railway Guide* and the Book of Genesis in Arabic, a map of London, a shilling razor, a child's feeding bottle, a box of cigars, daily and weekly newspapers, a set of British currency and one Indian rupee, a scale model of the obelisk in bronze, a hydraulic jack and pictures of twelve of the prettiest English women.

The Royal Festival Hall

London has a number of concert halls, the most famous of which is probably the Albert Hall. Far better architecturally and acoustically is the Royal Festival Hall, built in 1951 as part of the Festival of Britain and today the only major surviving component from that famous Thames-side exhibition. The centre of the South Bank arts complex, it was designed for the London County Council by Robert Matthew and J. L. Martin and is now widely accepted as London's best building from the 1950s. Architecture apart, it is also one of the world's most successful and best loved concert halls. In front is the embankment promenade and the floating Festival Pier, a stopping point for the river's fleets of pleasure and trip boats. Behind are the blank stone-faced blocks built originally as offices for Shell Petroleum but recently converted into flats.

The Victoria Embankment

From Westminster to Waterloo the north bank of the Thames is flanked by the Victoria Embankment, the first of the embanked sections created by Sir Joseph Bazalgette from the mid-1860s. Separating the embankment with its main road and the range of predominantly governmental buildings is the long line of the Victoria Embankment Gardens, park-like in their diversity and filled with trees. These form a peaceful backdrop to the river, busy at this point with the comings and goings of pleasure boats. One, strangely disguised as a nineteenth-century Mississipi stern-wheeler, is moored in the foreground. Beyond is the Hungerford railway bridge, whose stark lines have been improved by colour, and behind that are the far more elegant arches of Waterloo Bridge, built in the late 1930s to the design of Giles Gilbert Scott.

Towards Blackfriars

The Victoria Embankment continues eastwards from Waterloo, its progress marked by the familiar Victorian bronze lamps with their delightful entwined dolphin supports. Originally made for gas, these are now electrically lit. The broad sweep of King's Reach continues towards Blackfriars Bridge, an iron structure of 1869. At one time there were three bridges in parallel here, with two carrying railways to stations at Ludgate Hill, Holborn Viaduct and Blackfriars. In those heady, ambitious Victorian days, trains from Blackfriars were the start of journeys to Cannes, Brindisi, Dresden, St Petersburg and other exotic destinations. Today, only one bridge remains, and that carries commuters from south London towards their office desks in the city. In this picture the two tall towers are the soaring chimney of the former Bankside power station and, in the distance, Canary Wharf.

FARADAY

MICHAEL FARADAY
SEPTEMBER 22ND 1791
AUGUST 25TH 1867

DISCOVERY OF ELECTRO
MAGNETIC INDUCTION
AUGUST 29TH 1831

Michael Faraday

London is richly endowed with statues of the great, the good and the largely forgotten, with the earliest dating from the seventeenth century. Inevitably, the vast majority date from the Victorian and Edwardian eras, and there is a fine collection of these in the Victoria Embankment Gardens, one of London's greatest and least known sculpture parks. Here are heroes as diverse as General Gordon, Samuel Plimsoll, William Tyndale, Robert Burns and Sir Arthur Sullivan. The fashion for erecting statues has now rather passed, but very occasionally new arrivals are added to the ranks. One of the more surprising of these is Michael Faraday, the great Victorian electrical engineer and experimental scientist. His statue, a modern bronze cast from an earlier marble by John Foley, was finally erected on to his plinth in 1989 at the instigation of the Institute of Electrical Engineers, outside their headquarters in Savoy Place.

The Tower of London

Probably the most important example of early military architecture in Britain, and seen at its best from the river, the Tower of London has been in use as a fortress, a palace and a prison since the time of William the Conqueror. The White Tower, the central rectangular keep, dates from 1078 and has walls up to fifteen feet thick. It has three main storeys; the garrison floor; the banqueting floor with its Norman chapel; and above that the state floor with the council chamber and the Royal apartments. In this building Ann Boleyn was tried, Guy Fawkes was imprisoned, and Charles of Orleans, the father of Louis XII and the king of France was held hostage for a lonely twenty-five years following his capture at the Battle of Agincourt. The Tower's appearance today owes much to Sir Christopher Wren's restoration work in the 1660s. Still staffed by its Beefeater warders, the Tower and its riverside gardens are perennially popular.

Thames Shipping

London's docks, which flanked the Thames from Tower Bridge eastwards to Woolwich, were once among the busiest in the world, and the coming and goings of large ships filled the river with a continual traffic of tugs, barges, lighters, coasters and launches. Closed progressively from the 1960s, the docks have now disappeared, taking with them much of the river's commercial life. Tugs still work the river, sometimes hauling the traditional double-ended lighters, but they are mostly now engaged in the endless task of removing London's mountains of rubbish, much of which is moved by water. It is pleasing to see that these sturdy workhorses, sometimes drab and sometimes colourful, are still an important part of the Thames scene, and the sight of a tug at the head of a line of barges fighting its way against the fast flowing tide is as exciting as ever.

HMS *Belfast* and Tower Bridge

When it was opened in 1894, Tower Bridge was one of the mechanical wonders of the world. When its bascules, or drawbridges, are raised there is 140 feet of clearance between the river and the high, elevated walkway that links the two Gothic towers. Until the closure of the docks and the ending of commercial traffic in the Pool of London, these were in continual use. Today their opening is a rare phenomenon, prompted usually by the visit of some unusual vessel, a tall ship, for example, or a foreign warship. If the latter, this will usually be moored alongside HMS *Belfast*, the last surviving example in Britain of a big gun warship. This famous cruiser, whose six-inch guns often fired in anger during the Second World War, took part in the D-Day landings and other key battles. On her retirement from the navy, she was preserved as a floating museum and installed in her present, permanent berth.

The Prospect of Whitby

The traditional character of the riverside in the East End, an accidental conjunction of gloomy great warehouses, boatyards, cranes and other indefinable structures, and ancient pubs, which formed a background to the ever changing pattern of funnels, masts and superstructure presented by the ships on the river, has gone for ever. Old photographs and the etchings of Whistler show what it was like. Now the warehouses have gone, or been turned into smart flats, but some of the pubs survive, famous drinking places remodelled and themed beyond recognition. One of the oldest on the river is the famous Prospect of Whitby in Wapping, right on the water and still half-hidden among towering buildings. Its patrons are now tourists and flat dwellers from the converted warehouses rather than lightermen and dockers, but some of the history and atmosphere linger on, despite everything.

Greenwich

Built on the site of the medieval
Royal Palace of Placentia, the
Royal Naval College was created
in the late seventeenth century
on the orders of William II as a
memorial to his wife, Mary.
Designed by Sir Christopher
Wren, and described by Macaulay
as, 'a monument, the most
superb that was ever erected to
any sovereign', the gloriously
formal and wonderfully balanced
Baroque buildings flank the
earlier Queen's House and offer
from the river one of London's
best vistas. Originally a home for
disabled seamen, it became the
Royal Naval College in 1873.
Inside there is much to be seen,
including the Painted Hall with
its Thornhill ceiling and the later
Neo-classical chapel. The naval
association with the building will
soon be ended, but Greenwich
will continue to flourish as a
centre of nautical interest, thanks
to the National Maritime
Museum and the *Cutty Sark*.

Greenwich Park

Behind the buildings of the Royal
Naval College and the National
Maritime Museum, a grassy hill
dotted with trees rises steeply.
This is Greenwich Park, originally
laid out for Charles II by Le
Notre. From the hill there are
magnificent views across the
roofs of eighteenth-century
terraces towards the great loop
made by the Thames as it rounds
the Isle of Dogs, that narrow
peninsular that separates the
Greenwich and Blackwall
Reaches. Over the last thirty
years this view has been radically
altered by the regeneration of
London's docklands as a
residential and commercial
centre. At the top of the hill is
the old Royal Observatory which
straddles the zero line of
longitude. It is now a museum
housed in a range of buildings
that include the original structure
designed in the late seventeenth
century for Flamsteed, the
Astronomer Royal.

Riverside Houses

The Romans first made London into a port, but the real period of growth was in the eighteenth century. Docks and shipyards were constructed, and patterns of international trade established that were to continue until the 1960s. Warehouses spread along the river's banks but every now and then little groups of houses, in terraces or randomly built, filled the gaps between the commercial structures. Many of these were owned by ship's captains who would return from long and hazardous voyages to spend brief periods of rest with their families. Built right on the waterfront, these houses kept them close to the river's turbulent life. Many of these houses were swept away by Victorian development but a few survived, often decayed and disreputable. Now, with their wonderful river views, these houses are treasured, and fearfully expensive to buy. Behind those modern picture windows dim echoes of the eighteenth century still cling to life.

The Last Warehouses

Since the 1980s a tide of regeneration has swept eastwards along the Thames from Tower Bridge, bringing back to life those riverside regions condemned to dereliction and decay by the closing of the docks. Gloomy old warehouses, especially those with good river views, have been turned into desirable, and expensive, flats. Demand has ensured that few have escaped the hands of the developer. This warehouse, apparently untouched since the last ship sailed from its quay, is, therefore, a great rarity, and a tangible link with a way of life otherwise extinct. The grandiose style of the building, with its great brick pilasters, its decorative window arches, and its old cranes and hoists, are reminders of those days of Victorian ambition and enterprise, a time almost beyond recall, when maritime trade was king and the Empire was the source of all wealth.

Docklands

The regeneration of London's docklands has been a great success story, creating, in effect, a new city whose boundaries reach from Tower Bridge to Greenwich. Old warehouses and dock buildings have been restored and converted to new uses, both residential and commercial. New and often architecturally adventurous structures have filled the gaps, and the docks themselves have been filled in or turned into marinas and leisure centres. The surviving relics of previous lifestyles have all but disappeared. Flats and offices have been followed by shops and shopping malls, and new transport systems have been built to provide easy access to hitherto remote and inaccessible regions. The backbone is the Docklands Light Railway, a completely automated and driverless transit system whose predominantly elevated route offers a continuously changing panorama of Docklands, such as that shown here.

Canary Wharf

Long retired from shipping duties, old cranes stand eternally at attention while in the background a much younger relative gets on with the task of rebuilding Docklands. Canary Wharf is the heart of modern Docklands, a huge complex of largely Art Deco-inspired commercial buildings that give the Thames' riverfront a hint of Chicago. Skidmore, Owings and Merrill was the architectural partnership responsible for the total scheme, but the central tower was designed by Cesar Pelli. With its 850-foot height, and its towering verticality, this building, the tallest in Europe, can be seen on the skyline from many parts of London, an alien intruder from America or the Far East, and yet strangely exciting. In its scale, ambition and architectural diversity, Docklands is the most radical, and the best, thing to have happened to London and the Thames since the Edwardian era.

Millennium Mills

After the excitement of
Docklands and the grandeur of
Greenwich, the Thames becomes
an industrial river. Factories,
warehouses, mills, chemical
plants and refineries line the
banks as the river winds its way
round Blackwall and into the
Bugsby Reach. To the south is
Woolwich, the setting for the
Royal Arsenal and the Royal
Naval Dockyard, the latter at its
peak as a major naval
establishment in the sixteenth
and seventeenth centuries. To
the north is Silvertown, backed
by the gaunt remains of
London's greatest docks, the
Royal Victoria, the Royal Albert
and the George V. This is a
region where the Thames is
without the conventional views
of fine buildings, but where the
banks are filled with
extraordinary, unexpected and
often exciting vistas. Typical is
the suitably named Millennium
Mills, a blend of Piranesian
grandeur and picturesque decay.

Thames-side Industry

Evening light turns the riverside
industrial clutter into a random
assembly of abstract shapes, a
strange and exciting geometry of
cylinders, rectangles, triangles
and cones made more dramatic
by the strong shadows thrown by
the setting sun. These modern
industrial complexes stand by
the river, but often have nothing
to do with it. Docks and quays,
now disused, line the banks,
pointless maritime relics for
industries based entirely upon
the land. In these broad reaches,
there is, none the less, still
plenty of traffic on the river. In
the foreground, a tug with its
typical high bow, plods along
against the remains of the tide,
dragging its set of container-filled
barges.

The Woolwich Reach

In certain conditions of light, the Docklands skyline, with the dominant Canary Wharf tower, turns London into some transatlantic, or even futuristic city. In front of the tower, and echoing in a strange way the shapes of the cranes that made the river live in the past, are the pylons built to support the Millennium Dome. These mark the beginning of a new spirit of regeneration for a region that bears the scars of a century of casual industrial and commercial development. Striding across the river is the Thames Barrier. It was near here in 1878 that the river's worst maritime disaster took place, when the steamer *Princess Alice*, with 600 people on board, sank after colliding with another vessel, the *Bywoll Castle*.

The Thames Barrier

Flooding has always been a feature of the Thames, caused by certain conjunctions of wind and tide with a river overfilled by winter rains. The Houses of Parliament were inundated in 1762 and 1791. The risks have increased in the twentieth century, partly because of physical changes to the course of the river and partly because London sinks at a predictable rate. In January 1928 the Thames poured over part of the embankment, drowning fourteen people and making 4,500 homeless. The great floods of 1953 spared London, but devastated the Thames estuary region. In 1965 a surge of water took the river to the very top of the embankment. In response to this increasing danger, a moveable barrier was built across the river at Woolwich. Between each of the futuristic piers is a gate that lies flat on the river bed, ready to be raised when there is a risk of flooding from the North Sea.

THE ESSEX SHORE

The new Dartford bridge marks the end of London's outward sprawl and introduces a new phase in the life of the Thames. The massive river now sweeps towards the sea between huge tracts of marshland, a low-lying landscape protected by great sea walls that have been raised continuously since the thirteenth century as London and its surrounding land sinks inexorably at the rate of twelve inches every century. Apart from areas of major industrial development, at Dagenham, Purfleet, Thurrock, Tilbury and Coryton, the Essex shore is wild, bleak and empty, with villages set well inland on higher ground. Even the industries have in their scale and totality a curious appeal and oil refineries are, frankly, exciting in their futuristic shapes and skyline. This is a shoreline of mudflats and seabirds, meandering tidal creeks, remote villages and farms and abandoned military installations, interspersed with areas of excessive and careless overdevelopment.

The river is busy with ships carrying containers to Tilbury and oil products to Thames Haven and Shell Haven, with pilot boats and tugs, with fishing boats and pleasure craft. From the land behind the sea wall the river is often invisible, and so these ships cross the low horizon, apparently sailing through fields, and among the roaming cows and horses. After Canvey's bungalows and crowded caravans, the Benfleet Creek and the Leigh and Hadleigh Marshes mark a welcome respite, a return to the emptiness, but soon the seven miles of Southend completely occupy the shore. It starts with Leigh-on-Sea, still, miraculously, a fishing village at heart, and spreads eastwards to Shoeburyness where the Thames turns into the North Sea amid a confusion of marshland, long sweeping beaches and the legacy of military exploitation. In between is Southend and the old-fashioned seaside, with the longest pier in the world striding out over a mile of sand.

The Woolwich Ferry

Until the nineteenth century ferries across the Thames were more common than bridges but not many survive today. One of the oldest, the Woolwich Free Ferry, was established in the fourteenth century on the basis of a Royal privilege. In 1889 this service was established on a regular basis, and large ships were introduced capable of carrying vehicles, goods and passengers. The Woolwich Free Ferry has been maintained continuously since then. Over many years it was operated by a fleet of ancient paddle steamers that became one of the sights of London before they were finally retired in the 1960s. Modern double-ended roll-on roll-off vessels of the kind shown here are now used, keeping alive a service, and a tradition, that is part of the history of the Thames.

Erith and Dartford

After Woolwich and Beckton the character of the Thames changes, with the river widening perceptibly as it enters the low-lying landscape of Essex and north Kent. Great tracts of marshland flank the river, separating towns and villages far from the water's edge. Extensive housing and industrial development have reclaimed much of the land, but interesting buildings can be seen, with old churches and halls indicating centuries of settlement. Indeed, this area has many Roman associations. The river's route through Barking, Halfway and Erith Reaches is remote, but industry is always present, notably the massive Ford car plant at Dagenham, established on its riverside site in 1928, and in the lines of electricity pylons that criss-cross the countryside.

Dartford Bridge

The dramatic and beautifully engineered Queen Elizabeth II suspension bridge, which carries the M25 high above the Thames, is the last on the river and is the latest addition to the variety of ways that vehicles can cross the water east of Tower Bridge. Apart from the Woolwich Free Ferry, there are also three road tunnels. The idea of a tunnel under the Thames' lower reaches goes back to the eighteenth century, but it was not until 1897 that the Blackwall Tunnel was finally opened to traffic. This was doubled in size in 1967, when a parallel bore was completed. Next came the Rotherhithe Tunnel, finished in 1908, and built on the site of an earlier attempt at tunnelling under the river by Robert Vazie which collapsed in 1808. The largest and most recent is the Dartford Toll Tunnel, driven 100 feet below the river and opened in 1963. There are also pedestrian tunnels beneath the Thames at Greenwich and Woolwich.

Tilbury Fort

The first fort at Tilbury was built in 1539 on the orders of Henry VIII but this was not a substantial structure. The present fort dates from the 1670s, constructed for Charles II at a time when there were risks of attacks by France and Holland. Indeed, it was already too late, for a Dutch raiding party had landed in July 1667 and destroyed part of Tilbury church. The fort is a functional but attractive building inspired by the designs of Vauban, the great French military engineer, and set so that its guns could command the river and prevent the passage of hostile craft. It has a splendid Baroque gateway, a triumphal arch enriched with carved military trophies in a notably French style. Barely altered by the Victorians during their wave of defence building, Tilbury Fort remains one of the best examples of this type of building. Today, the fort, bristling with more modern armaments, is enjoyably remote, in a marshland landscape with magnificent river views.

Tilbury

Set well to the east, Tilbury Fort has little to do with the modern town of Tilbury, a sprawling development that owes most of its existence to the docks. Opened in 1886 and initially unsuccessful because of their remote location, Tilbury docks came into their own as ships became larger. With good rail links the docks flourished and from the 1950s they began to take over from the traditional dock installations near London. Containers and changes in patterns of cargo handling finally killed off the London docks, and since the late 1960s Tilbury has been one of Europe's leading ports. Tilbury takes its name from two remote and ancient villages away to the east, one of which, West Tilbury, has associations with the first Christian mission to the Saxons in about 650AD. East Tilbury is where Englishmen gathered in 1588 to fight the Spaniards in case Drake had been unable to defeat the Armada.

Coryton

Beyond Tilbury the marshes take over the Essex shore, a bleak but interesting landscape that faces out over wild emptiness towards the wide expanse of the Lower Hope Reach. Little villages, Muckingford and Stanford-le-Hope, shelter inland. Then, with enjoyable suddenness, the oil industry takes over, filling the marshes with a futuristic landscape of tanks, pipes and flaming chimneys. The development started in 1876 when ships were forbidden to carry oil products beyond this point, and this soon grew into the huge network of refineries and storage installations that Coryton, named after the Cory brothers, Victorian oil entrepreneurs, represents. There are two sections, Thames Haven and Shell Haven, the latter taking its name from charts of Henry VIII's time and not from the petrol company. Together they present, when seen from the Kentish shore, an extraordinary vision of some city of the imagination.

Canvey Island

With much of its land reclaimed from the sea in the early seventeenth century by Dutch engineers, Canvey is an area of remote mudflats, astonishing suburban sprawl and caravans, with the sea kept at bay by strong defences. Much of the land is, in Dutch fashion, below sea level, and when the defences were breached during the floods of 1953, the whole of Canvey disappeared. Made into an island by the conjunction of three creeks from the Thames, the Holehaven, the Benfleet and the East Howe, Canvey is both exciting and horrific. The best part is to the west, a vast expanse of marshland and isolated mudflats, the province of fishermen and birds, made more extraordinary by a distant horizon of refinery tanks and chimneys. Two early seventeenth-century Dutch cottages survive, but the rest is modern and chaotic.

Fishing Boats at Leigh

Between Canvey and Leigh is Hadleigh Bay and Benfleet Creek. Inland, the ground rises steeply and suddenly, creating a dramatic bluff. Set high among woods are the ruins of Hadleigh Castle, wonderfully painted by Constable. In the Middle Ages Hadleigh commanded the land and the sea and was one of the most important castles in Essex. From Canvey eastwards to Southend and beyond, the Essex shore belongs to the fishermen, and has done so for centuries. Shrimps, cockles and all manner of sea fish caught by net and line have long been a staple product of the region. Many boats are still engaged in the trade but in Charles Dickens' time the numbers were prodigious. He recorded in 1888 'upwards of 100 sailing decked boats employed in trawling for shrimps in the Leigh district'.

Leigh-on-Sea

In 1805 two tiny fishing villages, Leigh and Prittlewell, stood in isolation on the wild Essex marshes. Ten years later the Essex coast had become a resort and in Jane Austen's *Emma* Mrs Knightly spent an autumn at South End: 'We all had our health perfectly well there and never found the least inconvenience from the mud.' The rest is history, and now the shoreline is completely built over for seven miles, from Leigh to Shoeburyness. Despite all this, and despite the ravages wrought by the railway and the roads which carve their way through its heart, Leigh-on-Sea is still, somehow, an attractive old fishing village. Indeed, it is the line of the railway that has isolated the old village and saved it from development. The boats are drawn up on the beach, and locally caught shellfish is still the order of the day.

Sailing near Southend

At Southend the Thames turns from a river into the sea, a huge expanse of water spreading away towards the distant Kent coast. With this transition come all the attributes of the seaside and all the pleasures, and pitfalls, of the traditional holiday resort. Southend and its coastline have been popular with Londoners since the late Victorian period, and that popularity continues today. Day trippers on trains and pleasure steamers were at the heart of Southend's success for years, but these are now history. The spread of commuting, the rise of the car and new attitudes towards the seaside and its pleasures have changed Southend. New leisure activities have taken over, with sailing at the head of the list. This is a common weekend sight on the beaches to the east of Southend.

Thorpe Bay

An eastwards spread of Southend absorbed existing villages, and created new ones. Thorpe Bay is one of the latter, owing its existence to the coming of the railway. Like most of Southend, Thorpe Bay has two faces. The first is the commuter town, with streets of expensive but dreary houses extending southwards from the railway, and a 1930s church. The second is much more exciting and represents the long-established appreciation by visitors of the fine stretch of beach that characterizes the local shoreline. Here is the old-fashioned English seaside writ large, a windy expanse of sand and seaweed broken by timber groynes, and backed by a delightful array of old beach huts stretching into the distance, facing bravely out to sea and offering the prospect of sandy fish-paste sandwiches and a warming cup of tea made on the primus stove.

Southend

Having been established as a resort, Southend was, in the 1840s, a fashionable town with grand hotels and handsome buildings, a population of under 2,000 and a regular steamer service from London. In the 1850s the railway arrived and that was the start of modern Southend. Rapid expansion brought a different type of seaside visitor and a burgeoning population as the town spread along the coast, gradually absorbing all the other seaside villages. Modern Southend is two things, a huge commuter suburb, and a delightfully downmarket seaside resort, full of fish and chips and traditional vulgarity. Its focal point is the pier, at over a mile the longest in the world, a length determined by the immense sand flats that appear at low tide. Opened in 1895, complete with railway, and subsequently rebuilt, the pier, and the town's 1902 Kursaal ballroom, capture the old-fashioned pleasures of the traditional seaside.

The Thames Sailing Barge

Still a familiar sight in the summer on the Thames estuary and in the harbours and rivers of the Essex and Kent coast, the Thames sailing barge is one of the most distinctive types of coastal trading vessels in Britain. Square-shaped, flat-bottomed, with its lee boards and large expanse of russet-coloured sails, carrying between 80 and 250 tons, and going almost anywhere with all kinds of cargo and only two or three crew, the sailing barge was the essential workhorse in these shallow, coastal regions. Developed in the mid nineteenth century from the traditional Thames lighters, the sailing-barge was at its peak in about 1900, when over 3000 were in service. Motor barges and the spread of road transport brought about its decline in the 1930s and only a handful were still trading under sail in the 1950s. Since then, a number have been preserved, reviving traditional sailing skills and the famous annual sailing-barge races.

Shoeburyness

On the empty beach at Shoeburyness there is nothing but water and sky. Ships pass and on the horizon a low grey shape is the distant Kent coast. This is the only indication that this wide expanse of sea might once have been something else, that it marks the end of a river that started as less than a stream all those miles away in Gloucestershire. Rising as it does near the Severn, the Thames almost divides England horizontally, and during its long course to meet the sea by the Essex marshes it has explored the heart of England. It is essential to stand on the beach at Shoeburyness to understand the significance of those dry stones in a field at Thames Head.

Shoebury

Two small villages, Shoebury North and Shoebury South, have existed here at least since the Middle Ages and both have early churches to prove it. Their quiet isolation came to an end in 1858 when the first gunnery ranges were established on the wild marshlands to the east, initially to test the new Armstrong guns against ironclad warships. Barracks and all the supporting military paraphernalia arrived, along with the railway, and Cambridge Town, a grid-like new development appeared between the Shoeburys. Since then the military influence has dominated an area that is still exciting in its wild isolation. This really is the end of the Thames, for after the rounded point of Shoeburyness there is nothing but the North Sea.

THE KENT SHORE

At first, the Kent shore is different, with smaller tracts of marshland backed by wooded hills and higher ground that at times comes right down to the Thames. Industry, in the form of cement, oil, papermaking and other things, is always present, but it is rarely all-encompassing, as on the Essex shore, and in between are real river towns and villages, Gravesend, Greenhithe, that still carry the flavour of the eighteenth century. These are places with strong maritime traditions, reflected by Greenhithe's long association with training ships: the *Arethusa*, the *Chichester*, the *Worcester* and others were moored here. East of Gravesend the marshlands begin in earnest, huge vistas of emptiness behind the sea wall broken by the flooded lagoons formed by years of clay extraction. This is a truly remote landscape, undeveloped and often inaccessible. Scattered farms and old towns and villages, Cliffe, Cooling, St Mary's Hoo, Allhallows, are set back on the hills, where the woods begin and the landscape changes dramatically and abruptly.

From Allhallows there is one of the best views in Kent, taking in the sweep of the marshes, the Thames and the Medway. This is Charles Dickens territory. He lived nearby and loved the remoteness and the sense of scale, both of which are still to be enjoyed. At the end of the Kent shore is the Isle of Grain, an extraordinary blend of emptiness, great vistas, the remains of old industries and military paraphernalia, failed tourist endeavours, and a massive oil refinery that fills the land and the skyline. Here, the Thames and the Medway meet, and flow together into the North Sea. At the river's very end is Sheerness, the northern tip of the Isle of Sheppey. For centuries a major naval dockyard and a town still filled with the architecture, and atmosphere, of the eighteenth century, Sheerness is, at the same time, a modern international port and a half-hearted resort, with the same bleak beaches facing out to sea as the Essex shore.

Gravesend

At its heart Gravesend is an old river port and fishing town, and there are plenty of echoes near the river of its seventeenth- and eighteenth-century past, despite the all-encompassing development of the nineteenth and twentieth centuries. It was here in 1617, on the eve of her departure for America, that Pocohontas died, and was buried in the riverside church. On the riverfront is the fine Victorian pier, now well restored after years of decay, and its pontoons busy with ships again. To the west of the town is an area called Rosherville, its name the only survivor of a huge and highly successful Victorian pleasure garden, equipped with a conservatory, a maze, a theatre and offering riverside walks and facilities for dancing and refreshments. First opened in the 1830s and greatly expanded by the coming of the railway and the steamer trade, Rosherville was an essential excursion in the late Victorian period.

Higham

In 1824 a canal was completed between Gravesend on the Thames and Strood on the Medway. Its route, designed to offer an inland journey for small craft that avoided a difficult passage, included a tunnel over two miles long. Never successful, the canal was later turned into a railway. Higham, previously a small and scattered hamlet, was greatly expanded to serve the canal. Later, it was further enlarged by industrial and suburban development, and a large jetty served shipping on the Thames. More modern industry includes clay extraction, and the riverside marshland is marked by flooded gravel pits, some of which are now used for sailing and water sports. The clay was used for the cement industry around Cliffe, a town high above the marshes with wonderful views from its early church.

Shornmead Fort

In the 1860s a National Defence Committee was established under the direction of General Gordon to make plans for the defence of England against the threat of invasion from Europe.
The Thames had always been a natural doorway to the heart of England, and it had been used by various invaders, notably the Dutch in the seventeenth century. General Gordon took the risk seriously and he instigated the building of a series of forts and other defence works. Two of these were built to command the Lower Hope Reach, a wide bend on the river before it narrows at Gravesend. On the Essex shore the fort was built at Coalhouse Point and on the Kent side at Shornmead. The two are similar in construction, a great stone curve of gun emplacements looking out across the river. By the end of the nineteenth century the forts were redundant, but they both remain to be explored. Shornmead is a dramatic ruin in an isolated setting, too solidly built to be demolished.

Kent Ports

The Thames' Kent coast is wild and undeveloped, a great expanse of marshland broken by creeks and mudflats, harbouring remote farms and overlooked by secret villages on the higher ground to the south. In earlier years the marshes were used for gunnery ranges and as suitable settings for munitions factories. There has always been industry since the area was made accessible by the railway, notably the huge oil refinery and storage facilities that dominate the eastern end of the Isle of Grain, on the mouth of the Medway. This was also the setting for an earlier port, an unsuccessful attempt to develop a new route to the continent and to America. Port Victoria, opened in 1884 by the South Eastern Railway, and named by permission of the Queen, was simply one of those grandiose nineteenth-century schemes that never got off the ground and, after its failure, its harbour facilities were absorbed into the oil terminal.

Sheppey

The river Medway joins the Thames by the Isle of Sheppey, a rather desolate and remote region that for years has been supported by the navy and a rather half-hearted tourist industry. Sheerness, commanding the two rivers, has always been strategically important. The Danes used Sheppey as the base for their attack on Essex, and Sheerness was a defence outpost in the sixteenth century. It became a naval town after the Dutch invasions of the seventeenth century, and by the eighteenth century it had grown into a substantial place. Fine terraces and other buildings still retain the atmosphere of that period. This was the setting for the naval mutiny of 1797, prompted by the appalling conditions in which ordinary sailors were forced to live. Tourism has also played a part in the development of Sheerness, and the town has for a long time had a big amusement park.

Sheerness Dockyard

As a naval dockyard in the eighteenth and nineteenth centuries, Sheerness was extensively equipped as a base for ship building and maintenance. In 1823 it became an independent construction and repair yard, following extensive redevelopment under the direction of the engineer John Rennie. The Victorian navy further expanded the dockyard and one of their great contributions was the boat store shown in the background here. Designed by G. T. Greene in 1858, this is one of the first multi-storey iron-framed buildings in the world. After a period of decline the navy finally left Sheerness in 1960. Since then, the dockyard and its facilities have been turned into a successful commercial port, fully equipped and well placed for the North Sea trade, small enough to offer ships a fast turnaround and supporting a base for pilot boats and a lifeboat station.

The End of the Thames

The beach at Sheerness marks the end of the Thames on the Kent side, as the river disappears into the wide expanse of the North Sea. Protected by his essential windbreak, a fisherman looks out towards the buoys that mark the channel for ships sailing to and from the docks at Sheerness and the Grain oil terminal. Far across the water is a similar beach, marking the end of the Thames on the Essex side.